The
Common Soldier
of the Civil War

The
Common Soldier
of the Civil War

BELL I. WILEY

CHARLES SCRIBNER'S SONS · NEW YORK

PRINTED IN THE UNITED STATES OF AMERICA
Library of Congress Catalog Card Number 75-18539
ISBN 0-684-14202-3

CONTENTS

The
Common Soldier
of the Civil War

Introduction

ROBERT E. LEE's biographer, the late Douglas Southall Freeman, once remarked that he regarded it a rare privilege to have lived for more than a decade in the company of such a great gentleman. In all his research, he said, he had never found evidence that Lee ever used an obscene or profane word.

Perhaps to their credit, the same cannot be said about the men who served under Lee, and Grant, and all the others. They were earthy, natural people in whose natures the fear of God was mingled with a healthy interest in the attractions of the world, the flesh, and the Devil. These common soldiers were the very heart of the America over whose fields and plains they fought the most tragic of American wars.

"Johnny Reb" and "Billy Yank" were more alike than not, despite their differing accents and obviously contrasting views on government. They were mostly farmers and rural people; they spoke the same language —and made it decidedly colorful thanks to a variety of words not found in General Lee's vocabulary; they cherished many of the same personal ideals and hopes; and they endured the same hardships and perils of soldier life. They disliked regimentation, found abundant fault with their officers, complained about the food, and hoped earnestly for an end to the fighting and a speedy return home.

A number of men in both armies were of foreign birth, newly come to America to escape the upheavals of Europe, only to find a greater conflict in their adopted land. Most, though, were native Americans, primarily farmers from the South, and more often city-dwellers from the North. They varied widely in age and education, but most were young, and the majority—particularly among the Federals—knew at least a few rudiments of reading and writing (though in some companies from the rural South fully one-half of the men could not sign their names to the muster rolls).

Outwardly their interests seem divergent. Northern soldiers were better educated, read more, and took a greater interest in public affairs and other news, the last largely because political campaigning went on in the Union while it languished in the Confederacy. On the other hand, perhaps because of their deeper ties to the simple life on the land, and because theirs was a

cause which demanded a high degree of faith, Confederates were more devoutly religious. Great revivals swept over both the eastern and western armies of the Confederacy in the last two years of the war.

But beneath these differences, Reb and Yank were the same, bound by one great common denominator: They all sprang from the lowly ranks of American society. They were America personified in all its human facets, and now at war with itself.

In the Civil War the common folk put themselves on record to an unprecedented extent because, for the first time in the nation's history, large numbers of them were separated from their families and neighbors. Absence from home impelled them to

Billy Yank.
Courtesy Wendell W. Lang, Jr.,
Tarrytown, New York.

4

write letters and keep diaries. Moreover, their novel and exciting experiences as soldiers aroused them to an unusual degree of expressiveness. So they wrote long and interesting accounts of their experiences and impressions, and in so doing, they revealed very much of themselves. As a rule the lowly people did not save personal documents, but because the Civil War was by far the most important episode in their humble careers, they preserved for transmission to their descendants the letters and diaries telling of their involvements in the conflict. These manuscripts, still available in great numbers in public depositories and in private possession, are a rich mine of information about the ordinary folk.

Johnny Reb.
Collection Stanley F. Horn.

Origins

OWING to the incompleteness of Civil War records (especially on the Confederate side) and the confusion caused by re-enlistments, the number of soldier participants has to be stated in approximate terms. The same is true of casualties, deserters, and prisoners. The aggregate of men who donned the Northern blue was about two million, while those who wore the Southern gray were roughly half that number. On both sides those who served at one time or another as common soldiers—that is, as privates and noncommissioned officers—comprised well over nine-tenths of the fighting forces.

Who were these common soldiers? Most of them were native Americans. A study of muster and descriptive rolls indicates that about 95 percent of Confederates and 75 percent of Federals were born in the United States.

The Irish Brigade celebrating St. Patrick's Day at Falmouth, Virginia, March 17, 1863. *Frank Leslie's Illustrated Newspaper*, April 25, 1863.

Of the remainder, the foreign-born soldiers, the Germans and the Irish were the most numerous, owing to the heavy immigration of those nationals in the decades immediately preceding the Civil War. Scattered through the Federal forces were about 200,000 Germans, 150,000 Irishmen, 50,000 Englishmen, 50,000 Canadians, and lesser numbers of Scandinavians, French, Italians, Hungarians, and natives of other countries. Some Union camps were a babel of tongues. One regiment, the 39th New York, had in its ranks natives of fifteen foreign countries, and the Hungarian commander, Colonel Frederic Utassy, gave orders in seven languages. The 15th Wisconsin regiment, made up largely of Scandinavians, had 128 men whose first name was Ole.

On the Confederate side the Irish were the most numerous of the foreign groups; their aggregate was probably between 15,000 and 20,000. The second largest alien group in the Southern armies were the Germans, who numbered several thousand. Other foreigners who had substantial representation among Confederates were Englishmen, Frenchmen, and Italians.

On both sides the foreign soldiers added color and variety to camp life. They sang their native songs, ate their native foods, and drank beverages popular in the countries of their birth. St. Patrick's Day was always a festive occasion in Irish units. The jumping contests, wrestling matches, boxing encounters, and horse races, which the celebrants staged, were enlivened by heavy draughts of whiskey (frequently donated by the officers), and before night guard houses were filled with inebriates, many of them suffering from blackened eyes, broken noses, bruised muscles, or fractured bones. Indeed, in some Irish units, St. Patrick's Day produced as many casualties as a major battle.

From Civilian to Soldier

THE overwhelming majority of soldiers on both sides were volunteers. The principal value of conscription, initiated by both Union and Confederacy in 1862, was to keep men already in uniform from going home, and to stimulate further volunteering.

After the volunteers signed up for service they proceeded to a nearby camp for completion of the transition from civilians to soldiers. Physical examination was a prescribed feature of induction, but in many instances medical scrutiny was so casual as to make it a mockery. Proof of perfunctoriness is found in the considerable number of women who, in fact, donned male attire, enlisted as men, and served for periods ranging from weeks to

Ho, for the State Service!
RECRUITS WANTED!
1ST PENN'A
CAVALRY,
FOR STATE DEFENCE!

Recruiting Office, Boston. Library of Congress.

years before officers discovered their sex.

The most amazing instance of masquerade was that of "Albert Cashier," a farm woman of Irish background who, in August 1862, at nineteen, enlisted as a private in the 95th Illinois. She served throughout the remainder of the war and in 1865 returned to civilian life, still posing as a man. In 1911, an automobile accident required her hospitalization, and it was then that her sex was revealed. In 1899 she had qualified for a pension, and filed with her papers in Pension Bureau Records of the National Archives is a report of three physicians who examined her at that time stating that she was afflicted with piles that were so sensitive as to "bleed on slight touch" but containing no indication that she was a woman. After her sex was discovered thirteen years later, pension authorities reviewed her claim; they were told

OPPOSITE.
Recruiting Poster.
Kean Archives, Philadelphia.

by one of her former comrades that "Cashier was very quiet in her manner and she was not easy to get acquainted with. . . . When I was examined for enlistment, I was not stripped, and a woman would not have had any trouble in passing the examination." The reviewers, convinced that Cashier had performed full service as a soldier, including participation in the Vicksburg, Red River, and Nashville Campaigns, recommended continuation of her pension; she drew it until her death in 1915.

After undergoing physical examination, however cursory, recruits were formally mustered into service. Many were inducted twice, first as state troops and a short time later as Union or Confederate soldiers. Induction into national service consisted of undergoing inspection (by companies) by the mustering officer, pledging allegiance to the United States or the Confederacy, promising to obey orders, and swearing to abide by the Articles of War, numbering 101, which were read as the concluding feature of the induction ceremony.

Recruiting volunteers. *Frank Leslie's Illustrated Newspaper*, March 19, 1864.

At some point in the transition from civilians to soldiers, the recruits chose their officers. As a rule the rank and file elected only their company officers (lieutenants and captains), who in turn chose the field grade officers (majors, lieutenant colonels, and colonels), but in some regiments soldiers elected all officers, including the noncommissioned from corporal to colonel.

Usually they perfunctorily elected persons who had taken the lead in raising the units. Sometimes, though, elections were hotly contested affairs, with competitors using promises, food, and liquor to promote their candidacy. Private A. Davenport of the 5th New York wrote his parents May 1, 1861: "The other night we held an election for 1st Lieut. Collins was our favorite but

A Yank who allegedly changed sex.
Frances L. Clalin: reputedly of the
4th Missouri Heavy Artillery and
13th Missouri Cavalry, Co. A.
Boston Public Library.

Volunteers at a camp for completion of transition from civilians to soldiers.
Photographic History of the Civil War.

Recruits in uniform, 21st Michigan. U.S. Signal Corps photo, Brady Collection, National Archives.

the officers of the Reg. wanted someone of their own class, in education, &c. Collins resigned in favor of Lieut. Hamblin, our Adjt. a fine man & a Scholar who was unanimously elected. . . . Hamblin made a very good Speech and invited us to join with him in a social glass of Brandy & water. The Col. [Abram Duryée] said that it was against the rules to allow any drink-ing, but as this was an especial occasion he would allow it."

Permitting men to choose their officers was a concession to new world individual-ism and democracy, and the consequences were often costly—men were chosen for many reasons other than their abilities as military leaders. This was true less often among Confederates than among Federals, because in the South's stratified society, recognized leaders generally raised units and got elected to office. Even so, some Confederate units had cause to complain of the ill effects of elections. Early in 1862 an intelligent and patriotic Mississippi lieutenant wrote his wife: "The want of capacity among our Company and Regimental officers is terrible. Some Captains cant read; others there are whose chirography would shame the heiroglyphics that bedeck the slopes of the Egyptian pyramids. Regimental officers are scarcely any better."

During their first days in camp recruits drew clothing and equipment. For Confederate privates, uniforms consisted of gray coat—double-breasted and hip-length initially but gradually replaced by a short-waisted single-breasted jacket (which gave Rebs the nickname "Gray Jackets"); gray trousers (throughout the war Confederate *Army Regulations* specified pants of sky blue color, but these apparently were never issued); cotton shirt of unspecified color; drawers; socks; shoes; cap (modeled after the French kepi); cravat of black leather; and double-breasted overcoat or "great coat" of gray flannel, fitted with cape. Uniforms drawn by Yanks in 1861 were similar to those of Rebs, the principal difference being the color, which for Federals was dark blue for coats and light blue for trousers. Union overcoats were single-breasted and blouses were of two types—a long

Confederate prisoners, with their guards, lined up for transfer to Northern prison camps. Library of Congress.

Private, Infantry, C.S. Army.
Kean Archives, Philadelphia.

Private, Infantry, U.S. Army Fatigue Marching
Order. Kean Archives, Philadelphia.

Corporal, Artillery, C.S. Army.
Kean Archives, Philadelphia.

Corporal, Cavalry, U.S. Army Full Dress.
Kean Archives, Philadelphia.

dress coat with high, stiff collar, and a short blue jacket, which was much preferred for field wear. On both sides uniforms were trimmed with colors indicating branch of service—red for artillery, blue for infantry, and yellow for cavalry. Mounted troops had shorter coats than the infantry, preferred boots to shoes, and wore trousers reinforced in seat and legs. Branch of ser-

vice was also indicated on the buttons of officers by appropriate emblems for ordnance and engineers, and letters A, I, and C for artillery, infantry, and cavalry. Buttons of Union enlisted men were adorned with a spread-eagle design; those of the Confederate rank and file contained the number of their regiment, except for artillery, whose buttons bore the letter A. In

Buttons from Army uniforms.
Collection *Civil War Times Illustrated.*

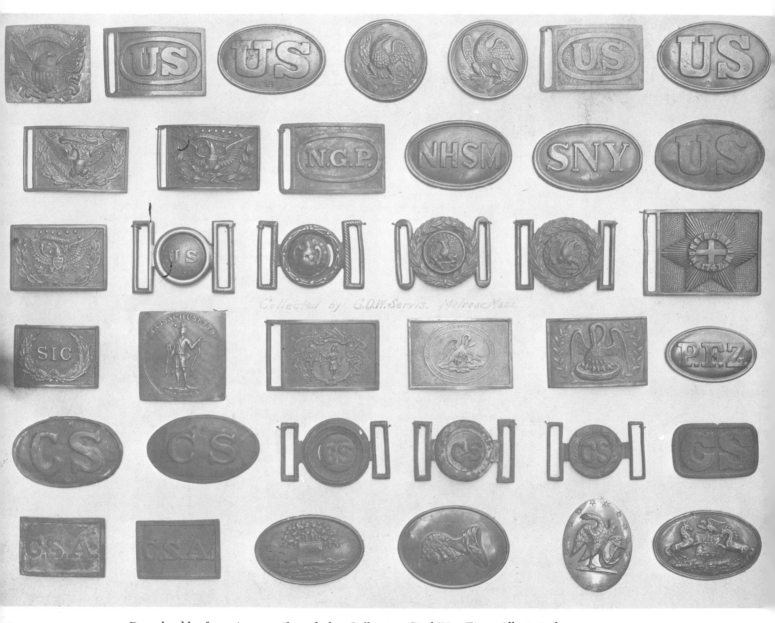

Brass buckles from Army uniform belts. Collection *Civil War Times Illustrated.*

both armies headgear was decorated with branch insignia and colors: Union officers and noncommissioned officers below the grade of general wore crossed cannon for artillery, a bugle for infantry, crossed sabers for cavalry, turreted castle for engineers, and flaming shell for ordnance, along with a brass numeral designating regiment and, when applicable, a brass letter specifying company. Union privates wore brass letters and numerals, the latter beneath the former, indicating company and regiment; on the

Confederate side branch was designated by the color of the cap crown.

Rank was also designated by trimmings and insignia. On the Union side the insignia, worn on shoulder straps, was virtually the same as that used in the U.S. Army today. On the Confederate side general officers of all grades wore the same markings—three stars in a wreath on the collar and four rows of braid on the sleeves. Confederate colonels wore three stars without the wreath; lieutenant colonels, two stars; majors, one star; captains, three bars; first lieutenants, two bars; and second lieutenants, one bar. Noncommissioned ratings in both armies were indicated by two or three chevrons on the sleeve.

In campaigns, soldiers were generally nonchalant in their observance of uniform regulations, and as recruits seasoned into veterans they became less concerned with appearance than with comfort. Rebs generally substituted soft hats for caps, and the shortage of commercial dye and factory-

Soldier group. Library of Congress.

Confederate prisoners on the way to the rear, captured by General Phil Sheridan
at Five Forks, April 1865. Library of Congress.

made cloth caused them to shift to garments spun and woven by relatives and friends and colored with homemade dye. Coats and trousers, dyed with the juice of walnut hulls, had a yellowish tint suggestive of butternuts; this distinctive hue gave to Rebs the popular nickname "Butternuts." Ties were worn by very few soldiers on either side; the general aversion to neckwear was reflected in a Reb's acknowledgment of a package from home: "I can put everything to advantag except the cravat—If I was to put it on the Boys would laugh at it." Drawers, generally ankle-length, were another item without

wide appeal. While they were used more often than ties, since they provided a safeguard against chafing of the flesh from rubbing of trousers on long marches, many soldiers, especially rural Rebs unaccustomed to undergarments at home, felt no need of donning them when they went to camp.

Both Yanks and Rebs who went to war in 1861 wore heavy leather belts fastened with brass buckles. Some of the buckles were of fancy design, but enlisted men generally wore simple types stamped "U.S." or "C.S." As the Northern blockade tightened, both leather and metal became so

Confederate cavalryman. Dragoon saber, 1840 pattern. Pair of 1842
single-shot pistols. Courtesy Herb Peck, Jr., Nashville, Tennessee.

scarce that most Rebs had to dispense with belts and use homemade galluses—or nothing at all—to hold up their pants.

Early in the war Rebs and Yanks normally carried extra articles of clothing—along with stationery, toilet articles, books, and photographs—in a knapsack. But in the course of campaigning most of them discarded their knapsacks and wrapped the contents, greatly diminished, in blankets draped from left shoulder to right hip and tied at the ends. Knapsacks made of canvas, rubberized cloth, or leather, and strapped to the back, were only one of several "trappings" with which new soldiers burdened themselves. Some took along to camp drinking tubes equipped with filters for use in sucking water from creeks and springs. Many Federals carried ponchos at one time or another, and Confederates appropriated for their use a considerable number of these raincoats.

Confederate soldier.
Courtesy Herb Peck, Jr., Nashville, Tennessee.

Confederate soldiers, prisoners at Gettysburg.
U.S. War Department General Staff, National Archives.

Equipment and Quarters

THE veteran soldier—Union or Confederate—considered himself well equipped if he possessed a blanket rolled in tent canvas or an India-rubber cover; a cloth or rubber haversack, known also as a "bread bag," which resembled an old-fashioned school satchel; a canteen, usually of canvas-covered metal, though those of Confederates were sometimes homemade wooden containers which had the appearance of flattened kegs (at least one Reb improvised a canteen from a gourd); a musket; a leather

Sibley tents—"shaped like a bell."
John Billings, *Hardtack and Coffee.*

cartridge box, loaded with forty rounds; a leather cap box; a bayonet in its sheath; a sewing kit; and mess equipment—hooked to the belt—consisting of metal plate, knife, fork, spoon, and cup, and sometimes a light skillet.

The weight of all this impedimenta ranged from forty to fifty pounds. Private A. Davenport, 5th New York, estimated the weight of his own equipment thus: "40 rounds ammunition, belt, &c . . . 4 lbs; canteen of water 4 lbs; Haversack of rations, 6 lbs; Musket, 14 lbs; Knapsack at least 20 lbs; besides the clothes we have on our backs." Most veteran Federals, and nearly all experienced Confederates, carried considerably less weight than this. Elimination of the knapsack and reduction

Interior of a Sibley tent,
showing gun-rack and stove,
with sleeper in customary
position, feet to center.
U.S. War Department General Staff,
National Archives.

OPPOSITE.
Inside an officers' wedge or "A" tent.
The chairs are folded flat for
easy transport. Library of Congress.

23

Tent interior.
Harper's New Monthly Magazine,
March 1867.

Negro soldiers outside a bomb-proof
of the 16th New York Artillery
at Dutch Gap, Virginia, 1862.
Ohio Historical Society Library.

Bomb-proof in Federal lines. Petersburg, Virginia, 1865. Library of Congress.

of its contents to ten pounds or less would produce a result that accorded more closely with established practice. Rare was the Southerner after the war's first year whose knapsack and food weighed six pounds. But even the lightest-traveling Confederate had to carry gun and ammunition, and he usually toted rations, water, blanket, tin cup and plate, and a few personal articles; all of these added up to about thirty pounds.

Shelter for Civil War soldiers varied con-siderably with time, seasons, location, and other circumstances. When the weather was balmy or the army on the march, the men often lived and slept under the open skies. Partly because of their prior mode of life and partly because of the Confederacy's limited resources, this unsheltered existence was considerably more common among Southerners than among their opponents.

The normal shelter, except in winter,

was a tent. In the first months of the war, Sibley and wedge tents were in common use. The Sibley tent, shaped like a bell (one Confederate wrote that "it looked like a large hoop skirt standing up by itself on the ground"), was supported by an upright center pole. Its ten to twenty occupants slept with their feet to the center and heads near the edge, like spokes in a wheel. Wedge tents, commonly known as "A" tents, because from the end they looked like a capital A without the bar, were pieces of canvas stretched over a horizontal ridgepole, staked at the ground on both sides, and closed at the ends. After 1861 the standard summer shelter of the rank and file was the shelter tent, widely known as the dog tent. In its most common

Wigfall Mess of the Texas Brigade at Seven Pines, Virginia, 1862. Library of Congress.

Beauregard Mess, "winterized" tent. Collection R. J. McDonald, Cincinnati, Ohio.

version this was a two-man habitation made by buttoning together the half-shelters and stretching them over a horizontal pole supported at each end by a pronged stick or a musket stuck in the ground with bayonet fixed. Occasionally three or four soldiers would combine their half-shelters to make a larger tent; and if a man wanted to go it alone he simply tied the corners of his canvas to the tops of four upright sticks and crawled under.

The winter quarters of most Civil War participants were log huts or "barricaded" tents. Logs of the huts' walls were horizontally laid after the fashion of frontier cabins or vertically arranged like those of a stockade. Cracks were daubed with mud and roofs were covered with boards or

27

Winterized tents. Old Print Shop.

Confederate huts built for winter quarters after
first battle of Bull Run. Library of Congress.

EQUIPMENT AND QUARTERS

thatch. Barricaded or "winterized" tents were made by superimposing wedge or shelter tents on log bases. Like the log huts, they were usually occupied by four men. Spaciousness and comfort were sometimes increased by digging out the earth floor to a depth of several feet. Tent roofs were waterproofed by stretching rubber blankets or ponchos over the canvas. Heat was normally provided by fireplaces built of sticks and daubed with clay. Chimneys, similarly constructed, frequently were topped with commissary barrels to increase the draft. Trench warriors, during the winter months, took to "bombproof" dwellings which resembled the dugouts occupied by soldiers of recent wars. (The number of soldiers involved in trench warfare in winter was relatively small until the siege of Petersburg and Richmond.)

Winterized tents, Army camp.
Copyright 1911, Patriot Publishing Co.

29

The Most Important Piece
of Equipment

THE most important item in Johnny Reb's or Billy Yank's equipment was his gun. Early in the war this was sometimes a shotgun, a squirrel rifle, a Tower of London musket (dating back to the War of 1812), a Belgian rifle (caliber .70), an Austrian rifle (caliber .54), or a Harpers Ferry Model 1841 (also called a Mississippi Rifle). But after 1861 most Yanks and Rebs were armed with Springfield (caliber .58) or Enfield (caliber .577) rifled muskets. These were cumbersome weapons, firing conical, hollow-based minie bullets, but they were sturdy, dependable weapons, accurate at ranges of 200–300 yards and ca-

pable of killing a man at a distance of a half mile or more. Some soldiers were equipped with breech-loading rifles such as the Sharps, Maynard, Burnside, Morse, or Star, and a few were fortunate enough to obtain seven-shot Spencer or sixteen-shot Henry repeaters. Cavalrymen usually were armed with short-barreled carbines.

In their letters Rebs and Yanks sometimes commented on their guns. They were sharply critical of the antiquated imports with which many of them were armed early in the war. A Wisconsin soldier described the Dresden rifles issued to his company as "miserable old things . . .

U.S. Springfield, Model 1855. West Point Museum Collection.

OPPOSITE.
Virginia infantryman with foot artillery model sword, Virginia manufactory flintlock rifle. Courtesy Herb Peck, Jr., Nashville, Tennessee.

Federal infantry privates. Right holds Enfield rifle, left holds
Springfield rifle. Courtesy Herb Peck, Jr., Nashville, Tennessee.

Federal cavalry private with saber and burnside carbine.
Courtesy Herb Peck, Jr., Nashville, Tennessee.

Rifle, English Enfield Model 1863. West Point Museum Collection.

U.S. Sharps box-lock breech loader. West Point Museum Collection.

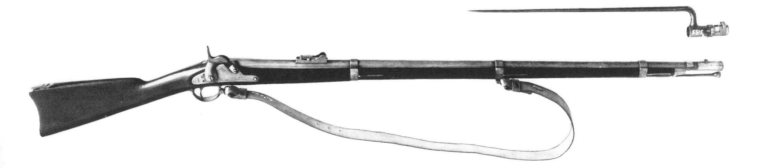

U.S. Remington, Model 1863. West Point Museum Collection.

[which] do about as much execution to the shooter as the shootee." A Hoosier private, who characterized his Belgian musket as "the poorest excuse of a gun I ever saw," complained: "I dont believe one could hit the broadside of a barn with them . . . the guns kick, oh my! no wonder they have check pieces in the stocks." Little wonder that soldiers referred to their outmoded muskets as "mules" and "pumpkin slingers."

Most Rebs and Yanks wrote approvingly of Enfield and Springfield guns. Concerning the former, one Yank stated: "We went out the other day to try them. We fired 600 yards and we put 360 balls into a mark the size of old Jeff [Davis]." Repeating rifles received the highest praise. A Mississippian whose company in 1862 drew five-shot Colt rifles informed his homefolk: "It is right funny to see the boys [of other companies] come over . . . to see our guns, take hold of them and say 'by golly boys if we all had guns like these we would clean the Yankees up in six months.'" A Connecticut soldier, whose regiment was armed with Spencer repeaters, wrote from near City Point, Virginia, May 19, 1864: "Our Reg't. has been under fire from the Rebs 8 days. . . . The Rebs made 3 charges on us but we stood up to the rack with our 7 Shooters & repulsed them each time & we piled the Rebs in heaps in front of us. The Rebs hate our guns they call them the Yankes 7 Devils. They say see the G. D. Yankeys stand up there with their G. D. Coffy mills wind em up in the morning run all day. . . . We are as good as a Brigade." (Some Spencers actually had coffee grinders incorporated into their butts.)

"It Comes Rather Hard at First to Be Deprived of Liberty"

In their camps, Rebs and Yanks had to adjust to a regimented routine that differed markedly from civilian practice. Life was regulated by drum or bugle calls, and these normally ran to about a dozen a day. The first was reveille, sounded at dawn or thereabouts, to rouse the men from their slumber and summon them to roll call. After lining up and responding to their names, they might be put through a brief and rapid drill, but usually they were left on their own until the second call about thirty minutes later hailed them to breakfast. The third signal shortly afterward sent the ailing to the regimental surgeon and the healthy to such fatigue duties as cleaning

quarters, policing company grounds, and cutting wood.

At guard mounting, sounded about 8 o'clock, the first sergeant of each company called out and inspected his detail for the next twenty-four-hour stint, and marched them to the regimental parade ground. There, to the accompaniment of music pro vided by the regimental band, the guards were formed into line, inspected by the adjutant, and sent off to their respective posts. The next signal was for drill, which frequently lasted until the call, sometimes known as "roast beef," announced the time for lunch.

After a brief interval of free time came another call for drill, which normally lasted one to two hours. Drill over, the men returned to their quarters, brushed uniforms, polished buttons and buckles, and cleaned their weapons in anticipation of the call to retreat which consisted of roll call, inspection, and dress parade. Both officers and men took great pride in the dress parade, held sometimes by regiment and sometimes by brigade, and always to the accompaniment of music.

The call to supper was sounded shortly after retreat. Then came another period of free time, after which tattoo brought companies back into line to answer roll. Upon dismissal the men returned to their quarters. The day was officially concluded by the sounding of taps, which signaled the extinguishing of lights and the cessation of noise.

Washing dishes, real soldiering
for a Confederate of 1863.
Photographic History of the Civil War.

OPPOSITE.
Soldiers washing clothes at camp.
Library of Congress.

Drilling a raw recruit.
National Archives.

This was typical routine for an infantry regiment during a period of quiet. Practices varied, of course, in different commands and with changing circumstances. Sunday routine was different from that of any other day. The big event of the Sabbath was a general inspection of personnel, equipment, quarters, grounds, kitchens, hospitals, and other facilities. Preliminary checks were made by the units' own officers. But the climax was inspection of the regiment by an outsider, usually the brigade commander or one of his staff. The inspector marched up and down the open ranks scrutinizing uniforms and arms, but he also poked into the knapsacks which the men had unslung, opened, and laid on the ground for his examination. Detection of

A 4th army corps division at
sham battle near Missionary Ridge, 1863.
Copyright 1911, Patriot Publishing Co.

Bayonet Drill, a typical temporary training camp. National Archives.

Squad cooking in camp. National Archives.

Drilling the awkward squad.
John Billings, *Hardtack and Coffee*.

Company K, 4th Georgia (Sumter Light Guards)
on parade, April 1861. They display
the earliest Confederate flag.
Georgia Department of Archives and History, Atlanta.

2nd Maine Regiment on parade, 1861. U.S. Signal Corps photo, Brady Collection, National Archives.

the smallest particle of dirt or the slightest deviation from uniform regulations was almost certain to bring sharp reproof from the inspector and a tongue lashing from the captain after return to quarters.

This inspection and the preparations that it required consumed most of the morning. "Knapsack drill," as the Confederates and Federals called the Sunday exercise, was an exhausting experience, and the soldiers of the sixties regarded it with dread. But like the other aspects of the regimentation

Camp of 31st Pennsylvania Infantry near Washington, D.C., 1862. Library of Congress.

of which it was a part, it helped mold undisciplined individuals into smoothly functioning organizations.

Many recruits complained of their regimentation. Charles H. Thiot of the 1st Georgia quoted approvingly a comrade's observation that "if he lived to see the close of this war he meant to get two pups and name one of them 'fall in' and the other 'close up' and as soon as they were old enough to know their names right well he intended to shoot them both, and thus put an end to 'fall in' and 'close up.'" A Louisiana Reb wrote from an Alabama camp December 25, 1862:

A soldier is not his own man. he has given up all claim on himself. He has placed his life in the hands of his superiors. he is as a checker player uses his men, if they see a chance to swap one for two they do it. I will give you a little information conserning evry day business. consider youreself a private soldier and in camp. you are not allowed to go outside the lines without a pass from your Comp commander approved by the cornel of the Reg. Well, you get youre pass more than once you go in some shop. in comes a guard with his muskett and says have you got a pass. you pull her out, she is all right. you go sauntering around and the first thing you know you are in somewhere where you have no business. you are very abrubly asked by a man with a muskett if you belong there. you very politely tell him you do not. he tells you to leave. you immediately obey or be sent to the guard house. you go back to camp. the drum beats for drill. you fall in and start. you here feel youre inferiority. even the Sargeants is hollering at you close up, Ketch step. dress to the right, ans sutch like.

Similar sentiments were expressed by D. P. Chapman of the 93d Illinois, who wrote from Camp Douglas in 1862: "They keep us very strict here, it is the most like a prison of any place I ever saw. There is a high board fence around the grounds and a guard also with muskets loaded. . . . It comes rather hard at first to be deprived of liberty."

The regiment. National Archives.

Diversions of Camp Life

REBS and Yanks found various diversions to relieve the boredom and deprivations of camp. One of the most satisfying recreations was singing. Soldiers of the 1860s were the "singing-est soldiers in American history, and the Civil War inspired more "sing-able" songs of the sort that endure than any other conflict. Letters and diaries indicate that the songs enjoyed most were "When This Cruel War Is Over," "The Girl I Left Behind Me," "Just Before the Battle Mother," and "Tenting on the Old Camp Ground," along with such old favorites as "Annie Laurie," "Auld Lang Syne," "Juanita," "Lilly Dale," "Sweet Evalina," and "Listen to the Mocking Bird."

Musicians of the 4th Michigan,
with snare drum and bass drum at the left.
The man at right wears musician's sword.
U.S. Signal Corps photo, National Archives.

Fort Moultrie Band. Brian Bennett Collection, Phoenix, Arizona.

Also rating high in camp popularity were the grand old hymns, "All Hail the Power of Jesus' Name," "How Firm a Foundation," "Rock of Ages," "Jesus Lover of My Soul," "Nearer My God to Thee," and "On Jordan's Stormy Banks I Stand." Patriotic and martial songs were sung with great gusto on the march and about the campfire. Top favorites of this category among Yanks were "Battle Hymn of the Republic," "John Brown's Body," "Happy Land of Canaan," "Gay and Happy Still," "Tramp, Tramp, Tramp," "Battle Cry of Freedom," "Yankee Doodle," and "Star Spangled Banner."

An old tintype showing Confederate drummer and fifer. Courtesy Herb Peck, Jr., Nashville, Tennessee.

Adam, the Minstrel.
Camp Life, vol. 33, September 1866.

Among Rebs "Dixie" and "Bonnie Blue Flag" ranked highest but great favor was also accorded "Maryland, My Maryland" and "All Quiet Along the Potomac Tonight." Perhaps the favorite of all Southern sentiments was the sweet and plaintive "Lorena." Both sides had their comic songs: Yanks favored "The Blue Tail Fly," "Shoo, Fly, Shoo," "Pop Goes the Weasel," and "The Captain and His Whiskers"; Rebs enjoyed these too, along with "Goober Peas." Without doubt the most popular of all songs

Confederate musician with
the long brass horn of that day.
Courtesy Robert W. Pawlak,
Los Angeles, California.

The Camp Minstrels.
John Billings, *Hardtack and Coffee.*

When their store-bought playing cards
wore out, soldiers made their own.
Courtesy Special Collections,
Emory University Library, Atlanta, Georgia.

119th Pennsylvania Infantry playing cards. Library of Congress.

Soldiers posed in boxing stance, Petersburg, Virginia, April 1865.
Brady-Handy Collection, Library of Congress.

A drummer boy and a first sergeant joking around at a card game.
U.S. Signal Corps photo, National Archives.

among both soldiers and civilians of the Civil War era was "Home Sweet Home."

Songfests were supplemented by instrumental music. Regimental and brigade bands provided music on ceremonial occasions and sometimes gave concerts in the evening. Informal groups entertained their comrades with minstrel performances fea-

Officers playing chess.
U.S. Signal Corps photo, National Archives.

turing stringed instruments. Almost every company had one or more talented violinists or banjoists who liked to render such rollicking tunes as "Billy in the Low Grounds," "Arkansas Traveler," "My Old Kentucky Home," and "Oh Lord Gals One Friday."

Another favorite diversion was gambling. Yanks and Rebs "shot craps" and rolled dice in a banking game known as chuck-a-luck, sweet-cloth, or bird-cage. Around campfires, at breaks on the march, and even while awaiting orders to advance in battle they brought out cards to risk their meager pay at poker, twenty-one, euchre, or keno. They also gambled on horse races, wrestling matches, boxing contests, cockfights, and louse races. When, in the Confederacy, paper shortage and dearth of funds made it impossible for Rebs to buy cards, they made their own, decorating them sometimes with likenesses of Jeff Davis.

In both armies religious men were shocked and grieved by the pervasiveness of gambling. A Mississippian wrote his mother shortly after a pay day late in 1862: "chuck-a-luck and Faro banks are running

Playing ball, camp of 13th New York heavy artillery, Petersburg, Virginia. Library of Congress.

Union officers and foreign observers study "Art of War" (the title of the book displayed). Kean Archives, Philadelphia.

night and day, with eager and excited crowds standing around with their hands full of money. Open gambling has been prohibited, but that amounts to nothing."

Early in the same year, John A. Harris of the 19th Louisiana wrote his wife, commenting specifically on two acquaintances with him: "This is the worst place [in] the

Nude.
Institute for Sex Research,
Indiana University.

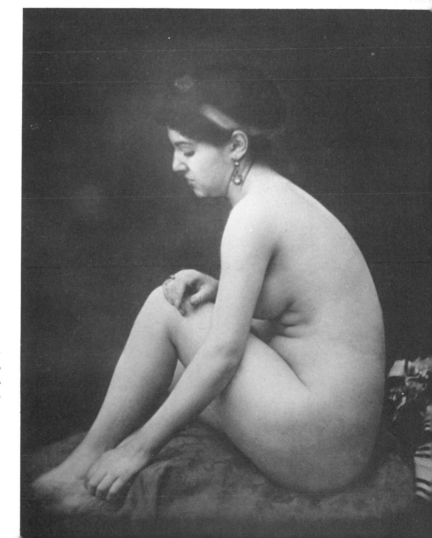

Nude.
Stenger Collection,
Institute of Sex Research,
Indiana University.

55

Showman in camp. Culpepper Court House, Virginia. Edwin Forbes drawing, February 11, 1864. Library of Congress.

world for men to get into bad habits. . . . I had no idea when I left home that Sullivan would ever Gamble, but he has done so. . . . John Dance . . . is playing cards regular, but dont play for money yet. He plays for Coffee and such as that. He is just now what I would call a student of Gam-

bling. I . . . have tried to shame him. At first he was Shigh about it but now he is bold."

Checkers, dominoes and chess also had their devotees, but were never as popular as card games. Both Rebs and Yanks played early versions of baseball, but the sports

Snowball battles among the Rebs often resulted in more casualties
than actual combat provided. *Battles and Leaders of the Civil War.*

Soldiers bathing. North Anna River, Virginia, May 1864. Ruins of Richmond
and Fredericksburg R.R. Bridge in distance. Library of Congress.

"Horseplay," Falmouth, Virginia.
Brady-Handy Collection,
Library of Congress.

Writing home.
Harper's New Monthly Magazine,
February 1868.

most commonly enjoyed were foot races, broadjumping, leapfrogging, boxing, and wrestling. In winter, snowball fights occurred, with participants battling in companies and regiments, under command of their officers. Prisoners were taken as in regular combat and when snow pellets were loaded with rocks or bullets, as was sometimes the case, painful casualties resulted.

Reading provided recreation for many. Newspapers and magazines were passed around in camp until they were literally worn out and the same was true of some books and pamphlets. Shakespeare, Milton, Hugo, and Dumas had some appreciative readers, but classic writers were far less popular than "Bill Arp," "Mr. Dooley," and the authors of Beadle's "Dime Novels" as well as paperback comics such as *Phunny Fellow* and *Budget of Fun*. Rebs and Yanks, like soldiers of other wars, also spent some of their leisure reading "racy" booklets and poring over pictures of nude or scantily attired females. Yanks, owing to their better pay and the more abundant offerings of Northern printers, had greater opportunity for indulging pornographic tastes than did Rebs.

In the absence of traveling troupes (the Hutchinson Family Singers, who toured the Army of the Potomac, was a notable exception) and organized recreational programs, Rebs and Yanks had to provide their own entertainment. Usually diversions were spontaneous and informal, but some units had enough initiative and talent to present theatricals of considerable merit.

Many Yanks and Rebs, and especially the younger ones, wrote friends back home about their amorous experiences with prostitutes and camp followers, and some spared no detail. One Reb even told what the fancy women of Petersburg charged him for their favors. But some soldiers stood fast against the devil's allurements. One of those was Private Orville Bumpass of Mississippi, who wrote his wife near the end of his service: "Uncontaminated I left home & so I expect to return."

Mail wagon of Second Army Corp.
Library of Congress.

Four soldiers relaxing.
Brian Bennett Collection, Phoenix, Arizona.

New York Fire Brigade Zouave imbibing liquid refreshment beside
a Temperance Society poster. Kean Archives, Philadelphia.

Crime and Punishment

Despite the diversions and sporadic entertainment, life in camp was for most a dull and dreary existence and breaches of discipline were frequent. Perhaps the most common offense was absence without leave, though liquor-inspired brawling ran a close second. Major General George B. McClellan early in 1862 declared that "drunkenness is the cause of by far the greater part of the disorders which are examined by the

Bending the elbow at a camp bar.
Library of Congress.

Stockade. Library of Congress.

courts-martial." A common offense frequently associated with drinking was insubordination. This usually consisted of enlisted men speaking disrespectfully to their superiors. One Yank, when placed under arrest, told his lieutenant: "You ain't worth a pinch of sh-t" and another, offended by a reprimand, said to the rebuking officer, "You kiss my arse, you God damned louse." A Louisiana artilleryman, annoyed by loud singing emanating from an officer's tent, shouted angrily "Shut up." Another Reb told a lieutenant who ordered him punished for disobedience, "No one but a damned coward would have a soldier bucked . . . if you will pull off your insignia of rank I will whip you on the spot." Rebs and Yanks applied a great variety of epithets to officers who offended them, including, "damned puppy," "sh-t-house adjutant," "bugger," "skunk," and "whorehouse pimp," but their favorite expletive was the time-honored "son of a bitch."

Another military offense to which the restriction and monotony of camp often contributed was desertion. Soldiers who unlawfully left the service aggregated about 100,000 Confederates and 200,000 Federals. On both sides hunger was also a factor in desertion; this was especially true of Confederates in the latter part of the war. "If I ever lose my patriotism," one Reb wrote his homefolk, "then you may know the 'Commissary' is at fault. Corn meal mixed with water and tough beef three times a day will knock the 'Brave Volunteer' under quicker than Yankee bullets."

Inadequacy of food also caused some of the theft and pillage that abounded in Northern and Southern camps. Soldiers stole money, watches, jewelry, and clothing from each other in order to obtain means for supplementing their meager rations. For the same purpose some roamed battlefields under cover of night rifling the pockets of the dead. Individually and in groups they scoured the countryside preying on helpless civilians and giving little if any consideration to whether their victims were friends or foes. Hungry soldiers repeatedly raided pig pens, chicken roosts, orchards, and gardens located near their camps, and

Camp punishment.
Courtesy Robert L. Kotchian,
Denver, Colorado.

Drumming a coward out of the ranks of the Army of the Potamac.
Harper's Weekly, June 28, 1862.

the propensity for "foraging"—the military euphemism for such depredation—was about as great in one army as it was in the other. Not all theft and pillage was motivated by hunger, of course; much of it had its origins in human depravity and the degenerating tendencies of army life.

Military authorities resorted to a great variety of punishments in an effort to maintain discipline. For minor offenses one of the most widely used penalties was confinement in the guard house, which usually was not a house at all, but a tent, a stockade, or a small plot of ground watched over by one or more armed guards. Confinement ranged in duration from a few hours to a month, depending on the seriousness of the offense; sometimes prisoners were limited to bread-and-water rations during all or a part of their incarceration.

Another common punishment was the wearing of a ball and chain. The ball was normally a cannon ball, weighing from six to thirty-two pounds, and it was attached to the leg by a chain two to six feet long. Culprits were required to walk about the camp, for varying periods, dragging the shackles behind them. A similar penalty was the carrying of a heavy object of some sort—a log balanced on the shoulder, a bag of dirt or bricks tied to the back, or a rock or cannon ball held in the hands—for repeated stints of one to four hours interspersed by brief periods of rest. This could be a painful punishment. A Texan told of a comrade who, for firing his gun in camp, had to carry a heavy log for three hours: "The first hour he done well, the second hour he was walking slow and looking serious and changing the stick from right to left and from left to right and calling for the time of day, and long before the third hour was out he was begging for mercy."

A corrective frequently applied by unit commanders was to force men to parade the company streets wearing large placards specifying their offense, such as "Coward," "Thief," or "I stole a skillet." A Union cavalryman had to walk up and down the parade ground carrying on his back a saddle that he had stolen. A Confederate who appropriated a citizen's pig had to wear the porker's skin around his neck in the presence of his comrades; and another Southerner who got the jitters while on picket and shot a dog had to lug the dead animal about the camp at double quick pace. A Confederate found guilty of selling whiskey in camp was placarded with the notice "Ten Cents a Glass," and ridden about the camp on a rail, with three bottles dangling from his feet.

Many petty misdoers were subjected to the humiliation of "wearing the barrel shirt." The barrel was fitted by cutting a hole in the bottom, so that it could be

Wearing the "wooden overcoat."
John Billings, *Hardtack and Coffee.*

slipped over the wearer's head, and by making openings in each side through which to pass his arms. Usually a sign indicating the misdeed was attached to the outside of the "shirt."

Other lesser punishments were assignment of extra guard duty (though some officers condemned this practice on the ground that it tended to degrade a responsible function intimately associated with soldierly honor); digging ditches; grubbing stumps; riding the wooden horse, a horizontal pole held aloft by two upright beams; standing on some conspicuous pedestal, such as a barrel, stump, or box; and cleaning the company grounds.

A penalty frequently imposed for insubordination was bucking and gagging. This

Bucked and gagged.
John Billings, *Hardtack and Coffee*.

consisted of placing the offender in a sitting position, tying his hands together and slipping them over his knees, inserting a pole or musket beneath the knees and over the arms, and tying a stick or bayonet in the mouth with a string. When prolonged for several hours, as frequently was the case, this was a terrible punishment. An officer who witnessed the bucking and gagging of a Federal artilleryman at Memphis in 1864 wrote afterward to his wife: "[after] 4 hours he was sobbing and crying as if suffering greatly. When untied he was not able to walk. . . . He was *carried* to his quarters."

Even more inhuman was the punishment, frequently meted out for "back talk," of tying men up by their wrists or thumbs with a rope thrown over a limb. Sometimes the victims were allowed to rest their full weight on their feet, but the general practice was to tighten the rope until only the toes touched the ground, thus placing a great strain on the wrists or thumbs and

causing the cord to cut into the flesh. Little wonder that men subjected to this torture after a while groaned and screamed in agony and that comrades, incensed by the brutality, angrily demanded their release and even cut them loose, sometimes at the risk of being subjected to the same punishment themselves.

A cruel punishment used in the artillery was to strap a culprit, with arms and legs extended in spread-eagle fashion, to the spare wheel carried on the rear of the caisson. If the vehicle remained stationary, and if the victim lay with his head at the top of the wheel for no more than an hour or two, the discomfort might be relatively mild. But if the wheel was given a half-turn so as to place the prisoner in a horizontal position, the time extended to several hours, and the caisson driven over rough roads, as was sometimes the case, it became excruciatingly painful.

The Federal and Confederate Congresses

Spread-eagled.
John Billings, *Hardtack and Coffee*.

A. R. Waud drawing of first military execution in Washington. The victim, a private, shot his superior officer. Library of Congress.

by acts passed respectively in August 1861, and in April 1862, prohibited the flogging of soldiers. But the injunction was sometimes ignored. Both North and South accepted branding as a legal punishment throughout the war, and courtmartial records show that it was widely used. The brand was usually the first letter of the offense committed—"D" for desertion, "C" for cowardice, "T" for thievery, and

"W" for worthlessness—and it was either stamped on with indelible ink or burned into the skin with a red-hot iron. The usual place of application was the hip, hand, forehead, or cheek.

Deserters, cowards, and other serious offenders sometimes were required as a part of their punishment to have half or all of their head shaved. To this and other penalties occasionally was added the provision that the victims be dishonorably discharged, stripped of their buttons and insignia, and drummed out of the camp. Drumming out was done to the tune of "The Rogue's March"—Confederates sometimes substituted "Yankee Doodle"—with soldiers in front and behind carrying arms reversed—in the presence of the regiment, brigade, or division to which the culprit belonged.

Another punishment frequently prescribed for serious offenses was imprisonment. Terms varied from a few years to life, and the place of confinement usually was a penitentiary or a military prison like the Federal "Rip-Raps" near Norfolk or the Dry Tortugas off the coast of Florida.

A few capital offenders (deserters, murderers, rapists, mutineers, spies, and the like) were hanged, but most soldiers who paid the death penalty were shot by firing squads. The shooting of soldiers was an awful spectacle, described in gruesome detail by many in their letters and reminiscences. The horror of these affairs was frequently enhanced by the clumsiness which required as many as three rounds of firing before the victims were finally put out of their misery.

Sleeping on sentry was a capital offense. Officers did a great deal of talking about its seriousness, and a considerable number of men adjudged guilty of dozing at their posts were sentenced to be shot. But the records do not show a single instance of a Civil War soldier actually paying the death penalty for sleeping on sentry.

Military execution by firing squad. *Frank Leslie's Illustrated Newspaper,* January 4, 1862.

Cleansing the Spirit

WHILE punishment was the principal reliance of commanders for combating crime and gross immorality, chaplains and the men to whom they ministered leaned heavily on religion to promote order and decency among the soldiers. In general the quality of Civil War chaplains left much to be desired, since the best ministers usually were reluctant to give up the security and comforts of civilian life for the uncertainty and hardship of camp. There were many notable exceptions, of course, among them such chaplains as John A. Brouse of the 100th Indiana and Charles T. Quintard of the 1st Tennessee.

Religious services, like diversions, were in large part provided by the soldiers themselves. Groups of them assembled on Sunday, usually in the afternoon or evening to avoid conflict with morning inspection, for preaching, singing, and prayer. Often the sermon was given by a company or regimental officer, or by one of the enlisted men. After listening to Colonel Granville Moody, a distinguished minister who commanded the 74th Ohio, a Yank stated: "It was one of the most eloquent sermons I have ever heard." Brigadier General William N. Pendleton, Confederate artillery chief, who at Manassas allegedly exclaimed while drawing a bead on the Yankees, "Lord preserve the soul while I destroy the body," often preached to his men. A sergeant who heard him speak in a log

The Reverend Charles T. Quintard, outstanding chaplain of the Confederate 1st Tennessee. Library of Congress.

Chaplain L. F. Drake preaching to the 31st Ohio at Camp Dick Robinson, Kentucky, November 10, 1861. Library of Congress.

tabernacle late in 1864, wrote afterward: "I never listened to more solemn and impressing remarks." When the military situation permitted, religiously inclined soldiers held informal week-day meetings, featuring prayers, testimonies, and songs. During months when the armies were in winter quarters, religious activities were intensified, with the result that great, emotion-charged revivals swept through the camps leading many sinners to repentance.

In some instances unit commanders led their men in prayer before taking them into battle. At religious services, and during intervals between worship, chaplains and colporteurs distributed tracts, made available in great quantities by church presses. These bore such titles as *Why Do You Swear?*, *The Gambler's Balance Sheet*, *Sufferings of the Lost*, *Satan's Baits*, *The Temperance Letter*, and *A Mother's Parting Words to Her Soldier Boy*. Both the tracts and the religious periodicals distributed in camp were widely read, not primarily because they aroused soldier interest but rather because of a dearth of secular books and papers.

The abundant exposure of Rebs and Yanks to religious literature, sermons, and prayers undoubtedly led to some improvement in discipline and morals. However, reform in most instances seems to have been limited both in scope and endurance. Certainly in most Civil War camps, the presence of evil was far more pervasive and persistent than righteousness.

"I Have Saw a Rite Smart of the World Sence I Left Home"

THE overwhelming majority of Rebs and Yanks were rural. Nearly half of those who wore the blue and well over half of their opposites in gray were farmers. Going to war was an exciting experience for men who rarely had traveled any considerable distance from the fields that they tilled. Private J. B. Lance, a rustic Tar Heel who went from his native Buncombe County to the environs of Charleston, South Carolina, in 1861, wrote back to his father: "I have saw a rite Smart of the world Sence I left home But I have not saw any place like Buncomb and henderson yet." Many of the rural soldiers got their first train ride en route to the fighting zone. Private Joseph H.

A nondescript group of rural Union recruits face the camera. Courtesy Herb Peck, Jr. Nashville, Tennessee.

William Black, the youngest soldier
to be reported wounded.
Photographic History of the Civil War.

Diltz, a farmer from near Urbana, Ohio, wrote a friend back home shortly after his long ride to Maryland over the Baltimore & Ohio Railroad:

Frank since I seen you last I hav seen the elephant. We started from urbana at three oclok p m. . . . we past within 4 mils of Whelling virginia. we past through some of the damdes plases ever saw by mortel eyes. We run under some of the god dames hills it was dark as the low regeons of hell We past through one tunel too miles long . . . as we was passing from tunelton to New Crick the cars run onto a stone that would weigh 500 lbs it was put on the track by rebels it was just whair the track runs close to the river if the engen had not bin so hevy we would hav all went to hell in a pile or some other seaport.

In age, Rebs and Yanks ranged from beardless boys to venerable graybeards. Charles Carter Hay joined an Alabama regiment in 1861 at age 11; when he surrendered in 1865 he was one month short of his 15th birthday. Little (if any) older than Hay was a Yank named William Black; his age and unit are unknown, but his picture plainly indicates that he was a mere boy.

The very young were usually drummer boys, though many teen-agers fought in the ranks as full-fledged soldiers. Perhaps the most famous of all the drummer boys was Johnny Clem of Newark, Ohio, who went to war in 1862, when he was 10. The smashing of his drum by a Rebel shell at Shiloh won him the name "Johnny Shiloh." At Chickamauga Johnny swapped his drum for a sawed-off musket and rode into battle on an artillery caisson. For gallantry in that fight he was promoted to sergeant and henceforth was known as "The Drummer Boy of Chickamauga." Soon after his promotion he posed for the camp photographer in a new uniform sent by some admiring Chicago women. In subsequent battles he was twice wounded and following the cessation of hostilities he applied for admission to West Point. When his application was refused, President U. S. Grant appointed him a second lieutenant in the Regular Army. He retired from military service in 1916 as a major general.

The oldest Confederate found among

hundreds of company rolls is E. Pollard, a 73-year-old man who, in July 1862, enlisted as a substitute in the 5th North Carolina. His military career lasted only three months, and he was sick most of the time. His discharge papers stated that he was "incaable of performing the duties of a soldier on account of Rheumatism and old age." Among Yanks, Curtis King, who enlisted at 80 in the 37th Iowa in November 1862, was almost certainly the oldest common soldier in the Civil War. One man older than he, William Wilkins, 83, donned the Union blue in 1862, but he was a major general, commissioned in the Pennsylvania Home Guards. King's regiment, known as "The Greybeards" and organized for noncombatant guard duty, was composed mainly of men over 45; 145 of them had passed their 60th birthday.

Most Rebs and Yanks were neither very old nor very young. On both sides 18-year-olds were the largest age group, and men ranging from 18 to 30 comprised about three-fourths of all the common soldiers.

Reports of unit commanders in the *Official Records* contain many citations of boy soldiers for gallantry in combat. At a critical point in a fight near Atlanta in July 1864, Eddie Evans, a stripling of the 24th Mississippi, seized the colors and, according to his colonel: "bore them with such conspicuous coolness and gallantry as to elicit the admiration of all. At one time he took his stand in advance of the line without any protection . . . distant from the enemy's line not more than fifty yards, waving his colors defiantly and called upon his comrades to rally to the flag."

Many of the boys paid the supreme price for their gallantry, among them "Little Giffen of Tennessee," whose death near the end

of the war, perhaps at Bentonville, was immortalized by the poet Francis O. Ticknor. Other youths, a larger number than were killed in battle, died of disease. On July 9, 1863, Private James K. Newlin of the 14th Wisconsin wrote from near Vicksburg: "Henry Cady is dead . . . 'Little Cady,' as we called him, was universally acknowledged to be the best boy in the Comp'y. . . . We all loved him dearly, now he is taken from us; he was always so good, kind, and accommodating, that every one who saw him took an interest in him at once." "Little Cady" had scores of counterparts in both armies.

Some of the boy soldiers attained high rank during their Civil War service. William P. Roberts of North Carolina, who enlisted in 1861 at 19, was promoted briga-

Johnny Clem.
Courtesy Herb Peck, Jr., Nashville, Tennessee.

Brigadier General William P. Roberts,
at 23 the youngest general
in the Confederate Army.
Photographic History of the Civil War.

Galosha Pennypacker. Library of Congress.

dier in February 1865 at age 23, and thus became the youngest general in the Confederate Army. On the Union side, Arthur MacArthur, father of General Douglas MacArthur of World War II, after winning the Medal of Honor at 18, for gallantry at Missionary Ridge, became colonel of the 24th Wisconsin; he led that valorous regiment with distinction through the bloody battles of Resaca and Nashville; after the war he rose to the grade of lieutenant general. Two other Billy Yanks who became colonels before reaching the age of 21 and who ably led their regiments in combat, were Henry W. Lawton of the 30th Indiana and John W. Forman of the 15th Kentucky. Galusha Pennypacker of the 97th Pennsylvania rose to colonel of his regiment and, one month before his twenty-first birthday, he was promoted to brigadier, the youngest general in United States history.

The boys matured rapidly in response to the challenges of marching and fighting. One of them, Private William W. Edgerton, who at 17 enlisted in the 107th New York in July 1862, wrote his mother eighteen months later from Chattanooga about his future aims.

It is strange how much a young man will learn from expeirance and study in a year and a half. one year and a half ago I dident have aney more calkulation than a last years birds nest, but haveing a great head or notion of studying human nature I have lernt a great deal, lernt to get all I can and ceep all I get, make as much out of every body as I can. I have no notion nor never did have, but I never untill now knew how to get around working all my lifetime, but now I know that buy working diligintly and not haveing aney holes in my pocket I neadent work very hard after I am 40 years old.

74

Triplets: George, John, William Brown. Courtesy Mrs. Ethel Reilly, Trumbull, Connecticut.

Most of the common soldiers on both sides were poorly educated. Illiteracy ran as high as 50 percent in many Confederate units, and the average was probably between 15 and 25 percent. Yanks were more literate than Rebs, owing to the North's superiority in educational opportunity for the masses. But even on the Union side, the company that did not have from one to a half dozen men who could not write their names on the muster roll was unusual. In both armies spelling and grammar left much to be desired. A Yank of the Army of the Potomac wrote shortly after Lincoln ordered that organization to be broken up into corps: "They are deviding the army up into corpses." Soldier accounts of camp illnesses led to a great diversity of misspelling. Pneumonia appeared in their letters as "new mornion," hospital as "horse pittle," erysipelas as "eri sipalous," typhoid fever as "tifoid feaver," and yellow jaundice

as "yaler ganders." One Yank who served under Brigadier General Frederick Lander wrote: "Landers has had the ganders but is getting well." An Ohio soldier informed his homefolk that he had been suffering from the "Camp Diary" and another Yank afflicted with the same malady wrote his wife: "I am well at the present with the exception I have got the Dyerear and I hope these few lines will find you the same." Surely this strange expression of hope was a slip of the pen. A Georgia soldier wrote his wife concerning his recent bout with diarrhea: "I have bin a little sick with diorah. . . . I eat too much eggs and poark and it sowered [on] my stomack and turn loose on me."

Francis M. Field of the 45th Ohio wrote his father in the fall of 1862: "the boys hant used wright; we have not drawed a cent of pay yet; we have to take it ruff and tumbel. . . . All the rest of the boys gits

George and John Brown,
Virginia.
Courtesy Mrs. Ethel Reilly,
Trumbull, Connecticut.

leters from home and i dont git any from home atall. . . . wright soon . . . excuse my poor writing and spelling . . . george huffman . . . has bin sick a good while [but] he is agiting better."

A Georgian stationed near Wilmington, North Carolina, wrote his wife: "This Countrie is so por it wolden hardle sprout pees." Another Reb informed his sister: "I will you send you my fortograph and [I] want yourn without faill." A third Confederate complained to his spouse: "We have to drink wate[r] thick with mud & wigel tails." Perhaps the champion misspeller of is "foad"; and verbs frequently are prefixed by the indefinite article as "the Yankies was arunning." Other speech characteristics which have a familiar ring to people who grew up in the rural South are exemplified by Malone's use of "a right smart force," of Federals, "we taken the turnpike," and "we will have a fight hear to reckly"— directly.

The three Warren brothers,
19th Battalion,
Virginia Heavy Artillery.
Museum of the Confederacy, Richmond, Virginia.

Young Union volunteer.
Courtesy Herb Peck, Jr.,
Nashville, Tennessee.

all those who wore the gray was Bartlett Yancey Malone of the 6th North Carolina. In his diary Gettysburg is "Gatersburg"; Blue Ridge is "Blew Ridg"; bean soup is "Been Soup"; adjutant is "adjertent"; bloody is "bludy"; some is "sum"; know is "no"; passing through is "passen threw"; peace is "peas"; tunnel is "turnel"; and missing is "misen." A cold day is a "coal day"; closer is "closter"; a court house is a "coat house"; where is "whar"; pretty is "pritty"; until is "untell"; accidentally is "axidently"; ford

Why They Fought

Individual motivation of the common soldiers varied greatly. Some had only vague ideas about their involvement in the conflict. Many signed up for service primarily because their friends and neighbors were enlisting. The prospects of release from family restraints and responsibilities, of travel, and of escape from the humdrum of farm and factory were tremendously appealing to the overwhelming majority of those eligible for military service.

Young Yankee soldier.
Courtesy Mrs. Ethel Reilly,
Trumbull, Connecticut.

Of Yanks, who in letters and diaries commented on their individual motivation, many indicated that their basic reason for becoming soldiers was to save the Union. They identified the nation of their birth, or their adoption, with liberty, democracy, social justice, and equal opportunity for all; they associated the South with aristocracy, preference for the privileged and suppression of the lowly; secession they viewed as unconstitutional, and armed resistance to national authority they deemed as traitorous. Typical of the sentiments of many Yanks were these expressed by 21-year-old John H. Stibbs of Cedar Rapids, Iowa, to his parents in Wooster, Ohio, telling of his reasons for volunteering as a private in the 1st Iowa. On April 18, 1861, six days after Confederates launched their attack on Fort Sumter, he wrote: "The majority of our Citizens are full of patriotism and express their willingness to stand by the old Stars and Stripes and protect it from dishonour. . . . Most of . . . [those few who expressed sympathy for the South] have had their ideas scared out of them and have come out for the government and the balance have been given to understand that

Young America can't tolerate a traitor and that they must come out and make a decided stand on one side or the other." The next day he wrote his father: "I did not ask the consent of you and Ma in my yesterday's letter as to whether you would be willing to have me voulenteer and I don't propose to do it now. *I take it for granted* I am doing right and that when my Country needs my services to protect her flag from dishonour and disgrace that my parents will be the *last* ones to object to my enlisting." Two days later he reported: "I have thought the matter over cooly and have counted the cost and if my life is needed for the defense of my Country I am ready to give it up, and do it freely." On April 23 he informed his father: "I am very anxious to get into action and am as ready as ever to go and do all I can even to giving up my life for the protection of the old Union that has given me and my Father our liberties and has made America the greatest nation in the world." Stibbs's subsequent service, during which he rose to the rank of colonel, proved that his patriotic utterances of April 1861 were not empty words, but expressions of deep-seated devotion to flag and country. At Fort Donelson, Shiloh, Tupelo, Nashville, and other engagements, he fought gallantly for the Union and not once did he express any doubt about the cause for which he repeatedly risked his life.

Yanks of foreign birth found the cause of the Union no less appealing than native Americans. On July 22, 1861, Philip Smith, a German immigrant member of the 8th Missouri, wrote in his diary:

As I lay in my bed this morning I got to thinking. . . . I have left home and a good situation . . . and have grasped the weapon of death for the purpose of doing my part in defending and upholding the integrity, laws and the preservation of my adopted country from a band of contemptible traitors who would if they can accomplish their hellish designs, destroy the best and noblest government on earth, merely for the purpose of benefiting themselves on the slave question.

Thousands of other foreign recruits expressed sentiments corresponding to those registered by Philip Smith.

Isaac and Rosa, emancipated slave children from the free schools of Louisiana. Library of Congress.

Some Yanks, though always a decided minority, were fighting primarily for the emancipation of the slaves. One of these was Chauncey H. Cooke, a young Wisconsin private, who wrote his father early in 1863: "I have no heart in this war if the slaves cannot be free," and who stated soon after the fall of Vicksburg: "I tell the boys right to their face I am in the war for the freedom of the slave. When they talk about saving the Union, I tell them that is Dutch to me. I am for helping the slaves if the Union goes to smash." Similar views were held by Urich N. Parmelee of Connecticut, who left Yale in 1861 "to free the slave" and who wrote after the issuance of the Emancipation Proclamation: "I do not intend to shirk now there is really something to fight for. I mean *Freedom.*"

Most Rebs who commented on their individual motivation indicated that they were fighting to protect their families and homes against foreign invaders. Some mentioned their concern for the growing power of the central government and the increasing impingement of Federal authority on state prerogatives as Northerners acquired the lion's share of the country's population and wealth. Charles E. Smith of the 32d Ohio, an emigré from the South, told in his diary of receiving a friendly letter from a Confederate cousin, in April 1863, in which the Reb stated: "I always thought some of . . . [my cousins] were in the [Union] army that was to crush this rebellion if it could but I do not think that it can, for although you have so many more men than we have, you have not those in power to manage things right. We are fighting for the Constitution that our forefathers made, and not as old Abe would have it."

Undoubtedly many Rebs were fighting for slavery, not so much as an economic institution, but as an established and effective means of perpetuating white supremacy, and members of the nonslaveholding class (to which about three-fourths of the Johnny Rebs belonged) were just as much interested in keeping the South a white man's country as were any other group in Southern society. As a general rule Rebs did not openly avow that their main reason for going to war was to uphold "the peculiar institution" but wrote instead of defending state sovereignty (under which they thought slavery would be more secure than under a national government dominated by Northerners) or "the Southern way of life." One Reb who forthrightly stated that he was fighting for slavery was Private G. G. Holland, a nonslaveholder, who wrote to a friend in September 1863:

You Know I am a poor man having none of the property said to be the cause of the present war. But I have a wife & some children to rase in honor & never to be put on an equality with the African race.

The Stuff They Were Made Of

ONE of the most notable traits of Civil War soldiers was their humor. Their sensitivity to the ludicrous and the spontaneity of their mirth gave them escape from their troubles and made the hardships of soldiering more tolerable. Rebs and Yanks liked to tease relatives and friends in their letters. Private William R. Stilwell of Georgia, after a year's absence from home wrote his wife: "If I did not write and receive letters from you I believe that I would forgit that I was marrid. I dont feel much like a maryed man but I never forgit it sofar as to court enny other lady, but if I should you must forgive me as I am so forgitful."

William Sprinkle, a North Carolina Reb, wrote a young married man of his home community: "Thomy I want you to be good and tri to take cear of the wemmen and childern tell I get home and we'll all have a chance. . . . I want you to go . . . and see my wife and childern, but I want

The 3d Kentucky (CSA) at mess before Corinth, Mississippi, May 11, 1862. Library of Congress.

Soldier. Courtesy Professor and Mrs. Dan Connell Moore,
Oxford College of Emory University, Oxford, Georgia.

you to take your wife with you when you go."

Private William W. White of the 18th Georgia, on April Fool's Day, 1862, wrote his cousin, from near Yorktown:

Camp Wigfall, Thirteen Hundred Miles From Any Place,
April, the one, 1800 & awful cold

Good Morning "Plug Ugly"

Your loving Epistle in which you vented all your spleen and heaped upon me all the base cognomens of which your ninny-head was master reached me. . . . I had hoped and prayed that when I entered the army . . . our associations would there be sundered . . . but it seems in that I am disappointed, for no sooner did you learn my whereabouts than you favored me with one of your soul-stirring, love-reviving, gizzard-splitting productions. . . . But you, Thomas, like all *long-eared ani-mules* would not stick to one side. . . . You need not blame me for not writing to you . . . [for] there is a little Blue-eyed Beauty in Georgia who writes to me every week and it consumes nearly all of my spare moments to answer her sweet and interesting letters; however, I expect to see you again in about fifty years provided I should live that long, and then I will tell you enough lies to last you one season. . . . Give my respects . . . to all inquiring friends and my wool dyed, double and twisted love to the girls.

Billy Yanks sometimes advertised for correspondents through the personal columns of newspapers. Some of these notices are obviously the work of mischief makers. The Chattanooga *Gazette* of March 6, 1864, for example, carried this advertisement: "Any young lady not sufficiently homely to frighten a dog out of a butcher shop nor sufficiently beautiful to bewitch the idle shoulder straps about town can get up considerable fun by commencing a correspondence with *Aaron*, Chattanooga Post Office." The New York *Herald* of March 8, 1863, under the heading "Matrimonial," printed this notice: "Two young gentlemen possessed of large fortunes, but rather green, wish to open correspondence with young ladies of the same circumstances with a view to matrimony—brunettes pre-

Negro Army cook at work, City Point, Virginia, 1864. Brady Collection, Library of Congress.

ferred—but no objection to blondes provided they are perfect past all parallel. Address Harry Longsworth and Charley B.B., Camp Dension, Ohio."

A Vermont Yank who had not heard from a friend in a long time wrote: "Ans[wer] this as soon as you get it and let me know w[h]eather you are alive are [or] not if you are dead I shall like to know it." And an Ohioan who lacked postage because of arrearage of pay wrote on an envelope addressed to his homefolk: "Postmaster please

A Government oven on wheels.
Photographic History of the Civil War.

to pass this through, I've nary a cent, but three months due."

In camp, fun-loving propensities were manifested in pranks and horseplay. Green recruits were sent to supply sergeants with instructions to demand their umbrellas, or were honored by election to the high but fictitious position of fifth lieutenant and then put to catching fleas and carrying water. Visitors who came to camp wearing stovepipe headpieces were hailed vociferously with such greetings as "Come out of that hat! I see your legs," or "Look out, that parrot shell you're wearing's going to explode." Wearers of shiny new boots were apt to be told to "Come up outer them boots; . . . I know you're in thar; I see your arms sticking out." Anyone who rode through company streets sporting an elegant mustache was almost sure to be hailed with suggestions to "Take them mice out'er your mouth; take em out no use to say they aint thar, see their tails hangin' out"; or, "Come out'er that bunch of har. I see your ears a workin'."

Civilians and dull-witted comrades were the usual victims of such horseplay. But officers, especially those who held staff positions, or who were incompetent, overbearing, or given to putting on airs, were considered fair game by pranksters. Indeed, soldiers were able when they set their minds to the task to ridicule intolerable superiors into resignation.

The humor of the common soldier was so irrepressible as frequently to manifest itself in battle. In one battle Rebel George Lemmon in his excitement fired his musket too close to comrade Nick Watkins' head shooting a hole in his hat. Whereupon Nick turned and said: "George Lemmon, I wish you'd look where you're shooting—I'm not

Piece of Army bread or hardtack.
Chicago Historical Society.

a Yankee." Many similar incidents occurred among the men in blue. In 1863 a Pennsylvania private wrote his homefolk, "We laugh at everything. . . . The roughest jokes I ever heard were perpetrated under a heavy fire."

At Chickamauga a chaplain who, as the shooting started, exhorted his charges to "remember, boys, that he who is killed will sup tonight in Paradise," was urged by a Reb to "come along and take supper with us." When the parson refused the invitation and galloped to the rear, a resounding shout went up from the advancing ranks, "The parson isn't hungry, and never eats supper."

Some of the best jokes were made about clothing and food. A Reb of General Joseph E. Johnston's army wrote from near Atlanta in June 1864: "In this army one hole in the seat of the breeches indicates a captain, two holes a lieutenant, and the seat of the pants all out indicates the in-

dividual is a private." Hardtack, the big thick cracker or biscuit which was the standard bread ration during periods of active campaigning, inspired many humorous sallies. A Kansas Yank reported the following camp dialogue:

SERGEANT: Boys I was eating a piece of hard track this morning, and I bit on something soft; what do you think it was?
PRIVATE: A worm?
SERGEANT: No by G-d, it was a ten penny nail.

The crackers were delivered to camp in barrels or boxes marked "B.C."—which probably was an abbreviation for "Brigade Commissary." But the consumers claimed with mock seriousness that the letters represented the hardtack's date of manufacture. "Teeth-dullers" and "sheet iron crackers" were other favorite designations for hardtack, and one Yank suggested that it "would make good brest works." The crackers were often so wormy that soldiers nicknamed them "worm castles," and one soldier stated: "All the fresh meat we had came in the hard bread . . . and I preferring my game cooked, used to toast my biscuits." A Yank, annoyed by the brevity of a letter he had recently received from home wrote back to the sender: "Yore leter was short and sweet, jist like a rosted maget."

The meat did no better. A Reb complained that the beef issued to him must have been carved from a bull "too old for the conscript law," while a comrade declared that the cows that supplied the meat for his unit were so feeble that "it takes two hands to hold up one beef to shoot it." Yanks also found much fault with their

Commissary Department of 50th New York. Library of Congress.

meat ration which they commonly referred to as "salt horse"; but their choicest remarks were directed at the hardtack which comprised their bread ration.

As should already be clear, another impressive quality of the plain folk was their ability to give colorful and forceful expression to their thoughts, and this despite the serious deficiencies of most of them in grammar and spelling. Some of their figures of speech were pungent and vivid. One Reb commented that "the Yankees were thicker [th]an lise on a hen and a dam site ornraier," while another reported that his comrades were "pitching around like a blind dog in a meat hous," and a

third wrote that it was raining "like poring peas on a rawhide." An Ohioan reported that Rebel dwellings near Fredericksburg looked like "the latter end of original sin and hard times," and another Yank wrote from Chattanooga that he was so hungry he "could eat a rider off his horse and snap at the stirrups."

Choice comments were inspired by the boredom and monotony of camp life. "You wanted to know how I like it," wrote an Ohioan to a friend; "i ain't home Sick i don't no What home Sick is but i no the diferens between home and Soldieren." Efforts to recount battle impressions and experiences also gave rise to vivid passages. An Illinois Yank reported after the Battle

86

of Jackson, Mississippi, that "the Balls . . . Sung Dixey around our years [and] the grape and Canister moed hour Ranks down like grass before the Sithe"; and a New York soldier wrote after the Williamsburg, Virginia, fight that "the air perfectly whistled, shrieked and hummed with the leaden storm." A Texan who was at Chickamauga noted in his journal that "if ten thousand earthquakes had been turned loose in all their power they could not have made so much racket."

Common soldiers of both sides achieved exceptional pungency in denouncing their officers. An Alabamian wrote his wife that "Gen. Jones is a very common looking man who rides just like he had a boil on his stern." Another Reb declared that his colonel was "an ignoramous fit for nothing higher than the cultivation of corn." A Floridian stated that his superiors were "not fit to tote guts to a Bear."

Yanks registered comments even more caustic. Private Hezekiah Stibbs of Iowa wrote his brother in January 1863: "We have got a good many officers in this regiment that never had a square meal untill they came into the service." Another Yank characterized those who commanded him as "woss than worthless." A Massachusetts soldier who seems to have been a prototype of Bill Mauldin wrote: "The officers

Fall in for soup. Library of Congress.

Fall in for soup.

This Union artilleryman displays a combination mess knife, fork, and spoon set. Courtesy Herb Peck, Jr., Nashville, Tennessee.

consider themselves as made of a different material from the low fellows in the ranks. . . . They get all the glory and most of the pay and don't earn ten cents apiece on the average the drunken rascals." Private George Gray Hunter of Pennsylvania declared: "If there is one thing that I hate more than another it is the Sight of a Shoulder Strap, For I am well convinced in My own Mind that had it not been for officers this war would have Ended long ago." But the peak of denunciatory expres-

siveness on either side was attained by the Yank who wrote: "I wish to God one half of our officers were knocked in the head by slinging them Against A part of those still Left."

In their home letters they made frequent mention of the elemental functions of nature. Some referred to diarrhea as "The Virginia Quickstep" or "The Tennessee trots," but more called it "the sh-ts." One Yank wrote his wife: "I expect to be as tough as a knott as soon as I get over the

Georgia Shitts," and another, heading his letter "Camp Sh-t," informed his spouse: "To tell the truth we are between a sh-t and a sweat out here." A North Carolina Reb wrote his wife concerning a comrade: "Marke Kelley . . . hant a friend in the company, it is thought that he will be put out of office for some misbehaveure with a woman on the cars and beter than all he shit in his briches and it run down his legs and filled his shoes."

An Illinois private wrote his wife early in 1862: "You say that our little Patty does not grow enough, well you must feed her well and give her lotts of 'titty.'" A Reb, annoyed by reports that neighbors were criticizing him for alleged misconduct in camp, wrote his spouse: "The people . . . that . . . speakes slack about me may kiss my- - -. . . . Mollie please excuse my vulgar language."

A third conspicuous trait was pride. The soldier's predominant fear when he faced battle was not that he would be maimed or killed—though concern for safety was very great—but that he might play the coward and bring disgrace on himself and his family. "I did not know whether I had pluck enough to go through [it]," wrote an Iowa Yank to his brother shortly after his baptism of fire at Fort Donelson, "but now I have no fear but I can do my duty, although I know the danger is great." A similar sentiment was registered by a Georgian who wrote his wife after his first fight, "it was a pretty severe anniciation . . . but thank god I had nerve to stand it."

On the day after the First Battle of Bull Run a Federal soldier wrote proudly to his father: "We got the worst of it but . . . I didn't run." And following the terrible fight at Franklin, Tennessee, in 1864 a Rebel informed his brother: "One of Old Abe's boys pluged me in the right foot making a severe wound, [but] I am proud to say that there was no one between me and the Yankees when I was wounded."

When deprivation, sickness, and war-weariness caused spirits to sag, pride in self and family kept soldiers at their posts. Private John Cotton of Alabama wrote his wife in May 1863: "I want to come home as bad as any body can . . . but I shant run away . . . I don't want it throwed up to my children after I am dead and gone that I was a deserter . . . I don't want to do anything if I no it will leave a stain on my posterity hereafter." And despite enormous hardship and anxiety both to himself and his family, he remained faithful to his cause until the end.

A fourth quality impressively demonstrated by the common soldiers of the Civil War was courage. This is not meant to suggest that all Rebs and Yanks were heroes, for there was a considerable amount of malingering, skulking, and running in every major battle. When Colonel John C. Nisbet of the 66th Georgia saw a soldier streaking to the rear in a fight near Atlanta in 1864, he yelled at the fugitive, "What are you running for?" Without slowing his pace the soldier shouted back, "Bekase I kaint fly." At Shiloh thousands of Yanks abandoned their comrades and took refuge beneath the bluff of the Tennessee River and at Chickamauga, when Longstreet broke through the Union lines, hordes of officers and men fled the field in panic. At Missionary Ridge a similar panic swept through Bragg's forces and Rebs ran en masse from the scene of action. But on both sides such conduct was exceptional.

The Civil War required more raw courage than most conflicts of recent times. For in that war men marched to battle in massed formation with a minimum of protection and supporting arms. Until the middle of the conflict they disdained to dig trenches and throw up hasty fortifications. Fighting was open, and closing with the enemy was more than a colorful phrase. Contests were decided by desperate charges in which muskets were fired at such close range as to burn the faces of contestants, and the climax was frequently a savage tussle in which men pitched into each other with bayonets, clubbed muskets, rocks, and fists. An Iowa soldier who took part in the fight at Allatoona Pass in October 1864 wrote: "When the battle was over one of our boys was found dead facing the enemy who had killed him. Both of them lay with their faces nearly touching . . . with their bayonets run through each other." This incident was by no means unique.

The desperation and the deadliness of Civil War combat is attested by the casualty rates. At Balaklava the Light Brigade, whose charge was immortalized by Tennyson, suffered a loss in killed and wounded of 36.7 percent. But at Gettysburg the 1st Minnesota and the 26th North Carolina each sustained a loss of about 85 percent. These were the heaviest losses of any regiments in any Civil War engagement, but the 1st Texas had 82.3 percent of its officers and men killed or wounded at Antietam, and the total number of regiments on both sides suffering losses of more than 50 percent in a single battle ran to well over one hundred.

In some battles the gallantry of common soldiers was so impressive as to inspire cheers from their opponents. History has recorded no greater displays of heroism than the Confederate assaults at Malvern Hill, Corinth, Gettysburg, and Franklin, and the Federal attacks at Fredericksburg, Kennesaw Mountain, Vicksburg, and Second Cold Harbor. In this last fight men of Winfield Scott Hancock's II Corps, when informed of the order to charge a seemingly impregnable Confederate position, wrote their names on slips of paper which they pinned to their uniforms so that their homefolk might be promptly informed of their fate. About fifteen minutes after the assault was launched three thousand soldiers of this battle-scarred organization lay dead or wounded on the field.

In the hard-fought contests of the Civil War innumerable plain Americans who ordinarily would have lived uneventfully and obscurely, without ever knowing the stuff of which they were made, attained the heights of heroism. Official reports of unit commanders which record the details of their gallantry tell of humble soldiers on both sides volunteering to perform perilous tasks, shrieking defiance at their foes, denouncing and even striking officers who played the coward, vying with comrades for the privilege of carrying the colors, taking over command when officers were all disabled, and refusing to leave the field when seriously wounded.

Two examples must suffice to illustrate the gallantry displayed by some of these noble men. Rebel Private Mattix, wounded so severely in the left arm at Murfreesboro that he could not wield his musket, went to his regimental commander and said: "Colonel, I am too badly wounded to use my gun but can carry the flag, may I do

Domestic scene in the camp of the 31st Pennsylvania near Washington, D.C., in 1862. Library of Congress.

it?" Private Mattix knew that carrying the colors was the most dangerous of all combat assignments. He also knew that three colorbearers of his regiment had already been shot down in that furious battle. But when the colonel nodded assent, Mattix seized the flag staff with his good arm, stepped in front of the regiment, and kept the colors flying through the remainder of the battle.

Near the close of the fight at Hanover Court House, May 27, 1862, a wounded Yank called out feebly to a regimental commander who was passing by. The offi-

Capture of a Confederate flag in the Battle of Murfreesboro.
Note flag of 78th Pennsylvania at left. New York Public Library.

cer turned around and stooped low over the prostrate soldier thinking that he wanted to send a farewell message to some loved one. But what the wounded man whispered instead was the inquiry: "Colonel, is the day ours?" "Yes," replied the officer. "Then," responded the soldier, "I am willing to die." And he did die and was buried on the field where he gave his life. This common soldier may never have heard of the Plains of Abraham and the heroic statements made there by the dying

Montcalm and Wolfe. But his words were as glorious as theirs and his valorous death deserves no less than theirs to be immortalized on the pages of history.

The greatness of this heroic Yank, of Rebel Private Mattix, and of their comrades who comprised the rank and file of the Union and Confederate armies was recognized and acclaimed by contemporaries. Joseph C. Stiles, a distinguished minister who accompanied Lee's army on the Antietam Campaign, wrote afterward to his daughter: "I could tell you a thousand thrilling incidents indicative of the glorious courage of our [common] soldiers." And he quoted a Federal prisoner as remarking: "A Confederate soldier! I believe the fellow would storm hell with a pen-knife." After the battle of Chickamauga a Confederate brigade commander, William B. Bate, reported: "The private soldier . . . [vied] with the officer in deeds of high daring and distinguished courage. While the 'River of Death' shall float its sluggish current to the beautiful Tennessee, and the night wind chant its solemn dirges over their soldier graves, their names, enshrined in the hearts of their countrymen, will be held in grateful remembrance."

In his official report of the Murfreesboro Campaign, Major General W. S. Rosecrans, after noting the splendid conduct of his officers, stated: "But above all, the sturdy rank and file showed invincible fighting courage and stamina, worthy of a great and free nation." A few days after Rosecrans made his report, Braxton Bragg, the commander who had opposed him at Murfreesboro, wrote the Confederate adjutant general:

We have had in great measure to trust to the individuality and self-reliance of the private soldier. Actuated only by a sense of duty and of patriotism, he has, in this great contest, justly judged that the cause was his own, and gone into it with a determination to conquer or die. . . . No encomium is too high, no honor too great for such a soldiery. However much of credit and glory may be given . . . the leaders in our struggle, history will yet award the main honor where it is due—to the private soldier, who . . . has encountered all the hardships and suffered all the privations.

Bragg's prediction that history would award principal honor to the private soldiers has not yet been borne out. The generals and political leaders continue to dominate writings about the Civil War. Bragg was right, however, in his appraisal of the character of the Confederate private. And what he said about Johnny Reb's individuality, self-reliance, and dependability was equally applicable to Billy Yank.

The Civil War was in large degree a soldier's war. In that struggle the determination, self-sufficiency, and endurance of the ranks were of utmost importance. Officer casualties were heavy, and in the hurly-burly of combat those who survived often were able to exercise little control over their units. In the crucial, climactic stages of battle the common soldiers were to a large extent on their own, and it was often their courage and tenacity, individual and collective, that ultimately decided the contest.

Still another trait conspicuously manifested by the common soldiers was a deep-seated devotion to duty. The words "honor" and "duty" appear with impressive frequency in their correspondence. The duty to which Rebs and Yanks generally seemed to be most sensitive was that involving their associates in arms. In general, they considered themselves honor-bound to perform their allotment of camp chores, to share equally the inconveniences and deprivations of army life, and to stand firmly by their fellows in the hour of peril.

The sense of obligation to comrades in arms found frequent and forceful expression in home letters. In 1863 a Mississippi private wrote his wife: "I have never had a mark for any neglect of duty Since I have been in the Service—and I dont intend that I ever Shall if it can be avoided." And he lived up to his pledge until honorably released by a Federal bullet at Franklin. In May 1864 one of Lee's soldiers wrote his mother: "I have been quite sick with fever for the last 4 or 5 days. They wanted me to go to Richmond but I am determined to see this fight out if it costs me my life." A similar sentiment was registered by an ailing Yank who, in response to his sister's inquiry if he had applied for a discharge, wrote: "I have not, and never shall. I would feel ashamed if I should succeed even in getting it . . . and I would love to join my Reg't soon. You don't know how sorry I feel I am not there now, as they no doubt will again be thrown into the fight with their decimated ranks, and share the *glory* with them. I really feel ashamed at my situation."

Duty to cause and country, while never as frequently expressed as obligation to companions in arms, was deeply felt by many soldiers of both sides. Many Rebs saw a parallel between the struggle that they were waging and that conducted by their Revolutionary forefathers, and when hardship weighed heavily on them, they derived much comfort from recalling the triumph over similar sufferings of Washington's army at Valley Forge. Shortly after the costly defeats at Gettysburg and Vicksburg, Sergeant John W. Hagan of Georgia wrote his wife: "I & every Southern Soldier should be like the rebbil blume which plumed more & shinned briter the more it was trampled on & I beleave . . . we will have to fight like Washington did, but I hope our people will never be reduced to destress & poverty as the people of that day was, but if nothing elce will

give us our liberties I am willing for the time to come." This humble man fought on in the face of increasing adversity, and when his lieutenant played the coward in the early stages of the Georgia Campaign, Sergeant Hagan took command of his company and led it heroically through fight after fight until he was captured in the battle for Atlanta.

Billy Yank's patriotism, like that of Johnny Reb, was a compound of loyalties to home and country. The dual attachment was forcefully expressed by Private John F. Brobst of the 25th Wisconsin in a letter to his sweetheart shortly after his unit arrived in Dixie early in 1863: "Home is sweet and friends are dear, but what would they all be to let the country go in ruin, and be a slave. I am contented with my lot . . . for I know that I am doing my duty, and I know that it is my duty to do as I am now a-doing. If I live to get back, I shall be proud of the freedom I shall have, and know that I helped to gain that freedom. If I should not get back, it will do them good that do get back."

On September 16, 1861, Samuel Croft of Pennsylvania, after a long march over difficult country, wrote his sister: "I did not come for money and good living, my heart beats high, and I am proud of being a soldier, when I look along the line of glistning bayonets with the glorious Stars and Stripes floating over them . . . knowing that the bayonets are in loyal hands that will plunge them deep in the hearts of those who have disgraced . . . that flag which has protected them and us, their freedom and ours, I say again I am proud and sanguine of success." Croft's patriotism was sorely tried by the mismanagement and reverses that bedeviled the Army of the Potomac

Battle of Stones River, or Murfreesboro, Tennessee. Sketch by Henry Lovie. New York Public Library.

for the next two years, but he served his country faithfully until he was shot down at Gettysburg.

Sergeant Edmund English of New Jersey, the son of an Irish immigrant, on January 8, 1862, wrote his mother: "Though humble my position is—gold could not buy me out of the Army until this Rebellion is subdued. A man who would not fight for his Country is a scoundral!" Sergeant English experienced periods of discouragement, but his shining patriotism always restored his spirit. In April 1863 he wrote: "The blind acts of unqualified generals and Statesmen have had no lasting impression on the motives which first prompted me to take up arms or chilled my patriotism in the least. I cannot get tired of soldiering while the war lasts. . . . As long as God

spares my health and strength to wield a weapon in Freedom's defense, I will do it." His life and health were spared, and when his three-year term of service expired in 1864 he reenlisted and fought on to the end of the war.

The sense of duty manifested by these men and countless others who wore the blue sustained the Union through the first years of bungling, gloom, and disaster. And when the expiration of the original terms of enlistment approached early in 1864, and the nation stood in grave danger because of the threatened loss of their proven courage, hardiness, and experience, they came forward by company, regiment, and brigade to pledge their continued service. By thus freely offering themselves for what they knew would be another season of

95

Voting in the field, 1864.

bloody sacrifice, they gave the nation one of its most glorious moments. To them and their kind the Union will ever owe an overwhelming debt of gratitude.

Another quality demonstrated by the common soldiers, blue and gray, was an enormous capacity for hardship. Because of their limited resources, Southerners were required to endure far more of suffering than were Northerners. But many Northerners experienced great misery, and when put to the test they bore their lot with no less fortitude than Confederates. Yanks on the Knoxville Campaign of late 1863 and Rebs at Nashville marched for miles over rocky, ice-coated roads in bare feet leaving traces of blood behind them.

Soldiers of both sides had their starvation times, though Rebs were far more intimately acquainted with hunger than Yanks. Many men in gray went for days without any food save a few grains of corn picked up from the places where the horses fed and parched over the glowing embers of their campfires.

The sick and wounded of both armies experienced enormous hardship, and in Confederate hospitals inadequate facilities, shortage of food, and dearth of medicine led to unspeakable agonies. Literally thousands of Rebs were subjected to the ordeal of having limbs sawed off without benefit of anesthesia. But the sick and wounded bore their miseries and tortures with remarkable courage and patience. An Alabama nurse wrote her superior from a Virginia hospital in 1861: "The fear that my *womanly* nerves would give way within the hearing of the 'groans of the wounded' almost made me shrink from the position I occupy, but while I grow sick at the sight of the amputated limbs and ghastly wounds, I must testify that a groan has rarely reached my ears and the heroism of our men has developed itself more thoroughly and beautifully in enduring bodily suffering . . . and want of home comforts that of necessity attaches to a war hospital."

Phoebe Pember, an administrator in Richmond's Chimborazo Hospital 1862–1865, in her memoir, *A Southern Woman's Story,* pays high tribute to the fortitude of the lowly patients. She relates in some detail the experience of a young soldier named Fisher, who won the admiration and affection of all those who came in contact with him by the patience and cheerfulness of his ten-month convalescence from a hip wound. On the night following his first success in walking from one end of the ward to the other, Fisher cried out with pain as he turned over in his bed. Examination revealed a small stream of blood spurting from his wound; a splintered bone apparently had cut an artery. Mrs. Pember stopped the blood flow with her finger and sent for the surgeon. The doctor promptly concluded that the severed artery was too deeply imbedded in the fleshy part of the thigh to be repaired.

When informed of the hopelessness of his plight the young man gave the matron his mother's address and then asked: "How long can I live?"

"Only as long as I keep my finger upon this artery," Mrs. Pember replied.

Then followed a silence broken by the simple remark, "You can let go . . ."

"But I could not," wrote Mrs. Pember in her memoir. "Not if my own life had trembled in the balance. Hot tears rushed to my eyes, a surging sound to my ears, and a deathly coldness to my lips."

"The pang of obeying him was spared me," she added, "and for the first and last time during the trials that surrounded me for four years, I fainted away."

Phoebe Pember, efficient administrator at Chimborazo Hospital.
Museum of the Confederacy, Richmond, Virginia.

Wartime photograph (April 1865) of Chimborazo Hospital at Richmond, Virginia.
Valentine Museum, Richmond, Virginia.

"I Can't Tell You How Bad
I Want to See You"

As previously indicated, love of family and home was one of the most notable attributes of the common soldiers, and this sentiment found frequent expression in their correspondence. The heartache produced by the severance of family ties was vividly reflected in the letters of Private William Elisha Stoker, a semiliterate Texan who spent most of his two-year service in Arkansas. In September 1862, about six months after leaving home, he wrote his wife Betty: "When I think of the pleasure that we have enjoyed and then think of the situation that I am now placed in, it almost breaks my heart. . . . I am constern[tly] dreaming about home. I am afraid I am

A very young Confederate
from Mississippi and his mother.
Courtesy Wm. A. Albaugh III.

Federal officer and his wife.
Collection *Civil War Times Illustrated.*

taken & brought with me. Betty Shew Priscilla my ambletipe [ambrotype] and write what she says about it." In February 1863, he informed Betty: "I dont know what kind of blessings I would have to come home & come walking up into the yard. . . . I think I must get about half tight to keep from Fainting when I get there, with over joy." He considered deserting, but when some of his comrades decided to go home and urged him to accompany them, he could not take this drastic step. "I told them no," he wrote Betty afterward, "[that] I loved my rib as well and would do as much as any boddy to see them [his family] on honerable terms but to desert and go it would throw a stigmey

going to hear something unfavorable." The following month he wrote: "I was in hopes some time ago that we would hav peace now. . . . I want to come home. I want to see you and [my little daughter] Priscilla. I can't tell you how bad I want to see [you]. . . . When you write, fill a sheet every time if you can and if you cant think of nothing, get Priscilla to say some thing and write it. You wrote that she was as smart & as pretty as ever. I wish I could see you & her. I am afraid that you & hers features I will for get I hav wis[hed] lots of times that I had of had your likeness

Zouave and his wife (or friend).
Courtesy Lewis Leigh, Jr.

Wedding photo of Major William A. Graham,
20th North Carolina Cavalry, 1864.
Courtesy J. A. Barton Campbell,
Charlotte, North Carolina.

Civil War Indian.
Courtesy Wm. A. Albaugh III.

Southern militiaman and his wife (?).
Modern photo by Herb Peck,
Jr., Collection of Fred Slaton, Jr.

100

Confederate soldier and his family.
Brian Bennett Collection, Phoenix, Arizona.

on me & her to[o] & it would be thrown up to Priscilla for years that her Par deserted the armey & wouldent fight for his cuntry. . . . I aint going to come home untell I can come like a white man. . . . I want to come so bad [that] I am nearley ded but that dont help the case any." Stoker apparently received a mortal wound at Jenkins' Ferry, April 30, 1864.

Stoker's distress at being separated from his family, extreme as it was, was exceeded by that of some other Rebs and Yanks. In May 1863, a Maine soldier stationed in Virginia wrote his homefolk: "I have seen men in the army [whose] . . . sickness and even death . . . was caused chiefly [by] discontent and homesickness."

Yanks and Rebs who were fathers repeatedly registered grave concern and deep affection for their children. Robert M. Gill of Mississippi wrote his wife Bettie in 1862: "I often ask myself whether our little Callie speaks of her Pa. Does she remember me? You must not whip her. I have a perfect horror of whipping children." Gill was exceptional in opposing whipping, because most fathers of his time sincerely believed that to spare the rod was to spoil the child. But his fatherly love had countless parallels in both armies. Some of the tenderest letters of Yanks and Rebs were addressed to their children. An Alabama soldier closed a letter to his wife thus: "I will say a few words to the Childern Willia I waunt you to Bee a good Boy and minde youre Mother Markus I waunt you and Willia to Bee smarte and make smarte men and all ways tell the Truth and mind what you are told and minde your'e Mother."

Innumerable Rebs and Yanks repeatedly urged their children: "Be good, mind your mother and dont neglect your books"; and this advice reflected the most earnest desires of humble folk for their offspring.

The Irish

Of the foreign-born soldiers in the Civil War, no group on either side won greater renown in battle than the Irish. Their response to combat was reflected in a letter that one of them, Felix A. Brannigan of the 76th New York, wrote his homefolk May 15, 1862, following the Battle of Williamsburg. "We were so close to the rebels," he said, "that some of our wounded had their faces scorched with the firing. . . . Fierce, short and decisive was the struggle. . . .

As we rush on with the tide of battle, every sense of fear is swallowed up in the wild joy we feel thrilling thro every fibre of our system." A month later, with more heavy fighting in prospect, Brannigan wrote: "I was never in sounder health or better spirits in my life. There is an elasticity in the Irish temperament which enables its possessor to boldly stare Fate in the face, and laugh at all the reverses of fortune . . . and crack a joke with as much glee in the heat of battle as in the social circle by the winter fire, or among boon companions at the festive board." At Chancellorsville on May 2, 1863, Brannigan won the coveted Medal of Honor. His citation stated that he "volunteered on a dangerous mission and brought in valuable information." His ability and gallantry brought him steady promotion from private to lieutenant colonel.

A glimpse of another Irishman's reaction to combat was afforded by Lieutenant Andrew J. O'Byrne's report of an engagement near Winchester, Virginia, in September 1864. "I took particular notice of a wild looking Irishman who stood near me," he stated. "He was loading and firing as fast as he could. . . . While loading and recit-

Brigadier General Thomas Meagher.
U.S. Signal Corp photo,
Brady Collection, National Archives.

ing some prayers in a jumbling sort of way . . . he would shout, 'Now Jeff Davis, you son of a bitch, take that,' giving his head a twist at the same time and his eyes looking wildly in front he repeated this several times til the front line was drawing near. We then ceased firing."

One of the most famous fighting units on either side during the Civil War was the Irish Brigade, recruited largely from New York City and commanded by Brigadier General Thomas F. Meagher. (One of the regiments of this brigade, the 88th New York, was known as "Mrs. Meagher's Own" because the general's wife presented the unit's colors just before it headed off for combat.) Before the brigade went into action at Malvern Hill, July 1, 1862, General Meagher made an inspiring talk to the men admonishing them to remember Fontenoy, where another Irish brigade had heroically fought for the King of France, and to remember that the eyes of Irishmen everywhere were upon them. The brigade gave a good account of itself in the fighting that followed.

At Fredericksburg, the Irish Brigade covered itself with blood and glory. By Meagher's order it went into action with every member wearing a sprig of green boxwood in his cap. It made repeated charges up the slope approaching Marye's Heights and each time encountered a murderous fire from Confederates posted behind the famous stone wall. An English correspondent of the London *Times* with Lee's army wrote: "Never at Fontenoy, Albuera or Waterloo was more undaunted courage displayed by the sons of Erin than during those six frantic dashes which they directed against the almost impregnable position of their foe."

The brigade went into action on December 13th with 1,200 officers and men; when it was formed on the morning of the 14th only 280 were present. This heavy slaughter virtually ended the career of the unit as a brigade. After the battle, when Confederates walked over the field, the dead soldiers closest to the stone wall were those wearing sprigs of green in their caps.

Confederates paid high tribute to the valor shown by the Irish at Fredericksburg. Major General George E. Pickett wrote to his fiancée December 14, 1862: "Your soldier's heart almost stood still as he watched those sons of Erin fearlessly rush to their death. The brilliant assault . . . was beyond description. Why, my darling we forgot they were fighting us and cheer after cheer at their fearlessness went up all along our line." Lieutenant General James Longstreet said of one of their charges: "It was the handsomest thing in the whole war." General Lee reported: "Never were men so brave."

On May 14, 1863, after Chancellorsville, Meagher, dispirited because of the diminution of his command, resigned. The remnant of the Irish Brigade, led by Colonel Patrick Kelly, took part in the fighting at Gettysburg on the second day. Here occurred a striking incident. When the brigade was ordered to fall in to reinforce the hard-pressed III Corps late in the afternoon, it was formed in close column by regiments. While the men waited in line, Father William Corby, brigade chaplain, stepped on a large rock and proposed to grant absolution to the men before they went into the fight. The soldiers dropped to their knees and uncovered their heads while Father Corby, with outstretched hands, pronounced the solemn words of

Father William Corby stood on this rock to bless the Irish Brigade
before they went into battle at Gettysburg, July 2, 1863.
Lane Studio, Gettysburg, Pennsylvania.

general absolution. He then urged the men to do their duty and acquit themselves bravely. He concluded by telling them that the Catholic Church refused Christian burial to those who played the coward. The soldiers then went forward and gave a good account of themselves in the hard fighting that ensued near the base of Little Round Top, and which resulted in the loss of one-third of their number.

In a number of engagements Union Irishmen fought Confederate Irishmen At Fredericksburg a Georgia regiment, mostly Irish, held the portion of the line at which the attack of Meagher's Irish Brigade was directed. When the Confederate Irishmen saw the green sprigs in the caps of the attacking Federal Irishmen, they cried out, "Oh God! What a pity we have to fire at Meagher's men."

Sometimes the Irish of the opposing sides singled out each other in personal combat. Major Robert Stiles in *Four Years Under Marse Robert* tells the story of a Confederate Irishman named Burgoyne of the 9th Louisiana who loved fighting so well that when infantry firing slackened he would attach himself to an artillery crew still in action and help service the gun. At Gettysburg, Burgoyne was acting as a cannoneer and screaming and jumping as he rammed home the charges. A recently captured Yankee Irishman standing on the other side of the gun was able to identify Burgoyne as a fellow son of Erin from his brogue. Disgustedly the Federal said: "Hey, ye spalpane! Say, what are yez doing in the Ribil army?"

Burgoyne immediately retorted: "Bedad, aint an Irishman a free man? Haven't I as good right to fight for the Ribils as ye have to fight for the [damned] Yanks?"

P. R. Cleburne.
Library of Congress.

The Federal Irishman replied: "Oh yes! I know ye, now you've turned your ugly mug to me. I had the plizure of kicking yez out from behind Marye's Wall, that time Sedgwick lammed yer brigade out o' there!"

"Yer a [damned] liar," said Burgoyne, "and I'll just knock your teeth down your ougly throat for that same lie."

Burgoyne thereupon leaped over the gun and took a swing at his opponent. The Yank was about to strike back when Stiles noted that his right hand was bloody and stopped the fight. On examination he found that the prisoner had lost two fingers before he was captured. When Stiles called the injury to the attention of Burgoyne, the latter replied: "You're a trump, Pat; give me your well hand. We'll fight this out some other time. I didn't see you were hurt."

The superb gallantry of the Irish is attested by the fact that on the Union side seventy-four of them—about 6 percent of the medals awarded, roughly equal to the percentage of Irish in the union army—won the Medal of Honor. Little wonder that a Union general who had first-hand knowledge of their battle performance in the Civil War stated:

If tomorrow I wanted to win a reputation I would prefer Irish soldiers to any other; and I'll tell you why. First, they have more dash, more *élan* than any other troops that I know of; then, they are more cheerful and more enduring—nothing can depress them. Next they are more cleanly. The Irishman never failed to wash himself and his clothes. Not only were they cheerful but they were submissive to discipline. . . . And confidence was established the moment they saw their general in the fight with them. . . . I repeat, if I had to take from 1 to 10,000 men to make a reputation with, I'd take the same men as I had in the war—Irishmen from the cities, the levees, the rivers, the railroads, the canals, or from ditching and fencing on the plantations. They make the finest soldiers that ever shouldered a musket.

The Indians

AMONG native Americans who donned the blue or the gray, the Indians were the most picturesque. Confederates recruited three Indian brigades, mostly Cherokees, Choctaws, Chickasaws, and Seminoles. One of the Cherokees, Stand Watie of Georgia, rose to the rank of brigadier general. The Union Army had one brigade of red men, most of whom were Creeks. Indian muster rolls located in the National Archives contain such interesting names as Privates James Sweetcaller, George Hogtoter, Crying Bear, Flying Bird, Spring Water, Samuel Beinstick, Big Mush Dirt Eater, and Bone Eater; listed among the Indian offi-

cers are Captain Spring Frog and Lieutenant Jumper Duck.

In combat, the red men performed well, though their tactics tended to be unconventional and officers had occasion to complain of their scalping their casualties. At Wilson's Creek and Pea Ridge the "Rebel Yell" of white soldiers was blended with the savage war whoop of their Indian comrades. In the Battle of Elk Creek or Honey Springs, fought in the Indian Territory on July 17, 1863, Yankee Indians fought Rebel

Group of Delaware Indians resting after a reconnaissance for the Union army. Kean Archives, Philadelphia.

Confederate Indian—Captain George Washington, Chief of the Caddoes. Smithsonian Institution, Bureau of American Ethnology.

Indians and commanding officers on both sides paid high tribute to the gallantry of their Indian units.

Between battles, the demeanor of the Indian soldiers left much to be desired. They were slovenly in dress, neglectful of camp duties, careless of equipment and indifferent to prescribed routine, especially that governing furloughs and passes. Colonel William A. Phillips, who was as well acquainted with Indian soldiers as any Union officer, observed that absence without leave was a "chronic Indian weakness." In his view: "The besetting sin of Indians is laziness. They are brave as death, active to fight but lazy."

The red men seemed inclined to support the side which appeared in strongest force among them, but this was no doubt due in large measure to two facts: first, few of them were deeply committed to the cause with which they were identified; and, second, they received shabby treatment from both the Union and the Confederacy.

Indian private of a Pennsylvania "Bucktail" regiment. Note the bucktail on his kepi.
Courtesy Herb Peck, Jr., Nashville, Tennessee.

The Black Soldier

THE discrimination experienced by Indians and foreigners was mild in comparison with that encountered by black soldiers, some 200,000 of whom served in Federal ranks. To begin with, the Negroes who offered their services to the Union early in 1861 were told that the government had no need of them. Not until early 1863, after combat, disease, and desertion had severely depleted Federal ranks, did Lincoln openly commit his government to the recruitment of Negroes.

From the very beginning black soldiers suffered much discrimination and abuse. Until June 1864 they received only about half the pay of their white comrades (black infantry privates, $7 a month; whites, $13), and their equipment and clothing were often inferior. The black troops were used mainly for cleaning camps, building defense works, and manning garrisons. In June 1864, the War Department issued a general order forbidding excessive use of black troops for labor and picketing. The order was widely ignored. In the fall of 1864, Colonel James A. Hardie reported after an inspection of the Department of the Gulf:

There are several Regiments of white Infantry . . . who have not yet been required to work a day since the receipt of this order, while colored troops have been required to work 8 hours a day. . . . The time which the colored troops would employ in drill and instruction is entirely taken up in performing not a share, but the whole of fatigue duty of the white troops.

A Negro corporal.
Courtesy Herb Peck, Jr.,
Nashville, Tennessee.

110

Recruiting poster for black soldiers. Library of Congress.

Cutting canal opposite Vicksburg.
Harper's New Monthly Magazine,
August 1866.

Frequently they were subjected to insults and brutal treatment by white officers and enlisted men. During investigation by a military commission of a mutiny of the 4th Regiment, Corps d'Afrique, in December 1863, a white captain angered by the brutality of Lieutenant Colonel Augustus W. Benedict toward black soldiers, testified:

I have seen him strike them in the face with his fist, kick them, and in one instance, strike a man with his sword in the face. On the 19th of October, I was officer of the day; the guard

was turned out for Lieutenant-Colonel Benedict and one man, Private Francis, of my company, did not dress properly, and Lieutenant-Colonel Benedict took the sergeant's sword and struck him in the face. I have frequently seen him at Fort Saint Philip, at guard-mounting, strike men in the face with his fist and kick them because their brasses were not bright or their boots not polished.

Another of Benedict's white subordinates told the commission:

On the 7th of August, at Baton Rouge, when officer of the guard, I was ordered by Lieutenant-Colonel Benedict to take 2 men, have their shoes and stockings taken off, and lay them down on the ground, straighten their legs and arms out, and stake them—tie them down. Then he told me to go to the commissary and get some molasses, and cover their faces, feet, and hands with molasses [thereby attracting flies and mosquitoes]. . . . the men had been stealing some corn to roast. . . . They were kept tied down from 10 a.m. until 7 p.m. or 7:30 p.m. They were tied down again the next morning. . . .

Benedict was sentenced to dismissal from service for "inflicting cruel and unusual punishment."

Typical of the attitude of many white Yanks toward their black associates was that registered by Lieutenant Charles H. Cox of the 70th Indiana Regiment in a letter to his sister, August 28, 1863:

I saw a *nigger* Brigade this morning [near Nashville]. . . . I do not believe it right to make soldiers of them and class & rank with our *white* soldiers. It makes them feel and act as our equals. I do despise *them,* and the more I see of them, the more I am against the whole *black* crew.

In spite of the widespread practice of restricting black troops to labor and guard duty, some of them got into combat. While evaluation of their combat performance is difficult, owing to the bias of much of the evidence bearing on the subject, it seems reasonable to conclude that they fought as well as the white troops with whom they served. No doubt some skulked or ran when subjected to the ordeal of battle, but the same was true of other troops, and especially those who lacked proper training or competent leadership.

In the Federal attack on Port Hudson, near Baton Rouge, May 27, 1863, two regiments of black troops, the 1st and 3d Louisiana Native Guards, numbering 1,080 officers and men out of a total force of 13,000, made six distinct charges over difficult terrain. The attack was repulsed, but the blacks won the commendation of Major General N. P. Banks for their meritorious performance. When Sergeant Anselmas Planciancois, a free Negro who carried the colors of the 1st Louisiana, fell mortally wounded during a charge, clasping the flag to his breast, two black corporals vied for the honor of carrying the standard onward. The contest was decided when one of them received a fatal wound.

At Milliken's Bend, June 7, 1863, near Vicksburg, when Confederates, numbering about 1,500, attacked a Federal garrison of about 1,100, most of whom were Negroes, some of the fiercest fighting of the war ensued. Captain M. M. Miller, a Yale senior who led one of the black companies, wrote his aunt after the battle that he lost fifty killed and eighty wounded in "the horrible fight" and that he had "six broken bayonets to show how bravely my men fought."

The valor of black soldiers was demonstrated again on July 18, 1863, when a Federal force of about 5,000 made a bloody but futile night assault on Fort Wagner, near Charleston, South Carolina. The assault was led by a black regiment, the 54th Massachusetts, whose colonel, Robert Gould Shaw, a personable young aristocrat, had followed the example of a fellow Bostonian (Thomas Wentworth Higginson, Colonel of the 1st South Carolina Volun-

A teasing comic valentine sent to an Ohio soldier in 1864 illustrates the strong racism in the North. Courtesy Mrs. William C. Pauley, Atlanta, Georgia.

You are a very nice young man,
And wish to wed, and think you can;
But what young girl would ever wed
With such a fright to go to bed?
You ugly, frightful, foolish elf,
I wonder you don't hang yourself;
You may weep both your eyes to brine
Before you get a Valentine!

Negro recruits for the 1st South Carolina (U.S.) drilling in
the streets of Beaufort. *Pictorial War Record.*

Storming of Fort Wagner by a black regiment.
Copyright 1890, Kurz and Allison.

J. L. Balldwin. Chicago Historical Society.

teers) in giving up the captaincy of an elite white company to assume command of a black regiment. Despite inadequate preparation for their assignment and difficulties resulting from darkness and rough terrain, the blacks went gallantly forward under heavy fire of rifles and artillery, supplemented at the peak of the assault by improvised hand grenades hurled from the fort by its defenders. One of the participants in the assault, Lewis Douglass, son of the renowned Negro orator, Frederick

Douglass, wrote that at this point in the action, "I had my sword blown away . . . [and though] swept down like chaff, still our men went on and on." After Shaw fell, shot through the heart standing on the parapet waving his sword and urging his men forward, the regiment fell back. Its 272 casualties exceeded those of any of the ten white regiments participating in the attack.

The day before the 54th Massachusetts suffered its costly repulse at Wagner, another black regiment, the 1st Kansas, played a conspicuous role in a Union victory at Elk Creek, in the Indian Territory. There a force of seven Union regiments attacked eight regiments of Confederates.

After two hours of stubborn fighting the Confederates were driven from the field. The Federal commander, Major General James G. Blunt, in his report of the battle stated:

Much credit is due to all of them for their gallantry. The First Kansas [black] particularly distinguished itself; they fought like veterans, and preserved their line unbroken throughout the engagement. Their coolness and bravery I have never seen surpassed; they were in the hottest of the fight, and opposed to Texas troops twice their number, whom they completely routed. One Texas regiment [the Twentieth Cavalry] that fought against them went into the fight with 300 men and came out with only 60.

The Statistics of Suffering

MORE service men lost their lives in the great conflict of the 1860s than in all other American wars combined, from the colonial revolt of 1775–1781 through the Korean War of 1950–1953. The approximate figures, in round numbers, are: deaths in all American wars, 1775 1953, except the Civil War—606,000; deaths in the Civil War—618,000, of which 360,000 were Union and 258,000 were Confederate, and of which approximately two-thirds came from nonbattle causes. Details are as follows:

A COMPILATION OF SERVICE DEATHS IN AMERICAN WARS *

WAR	BATTLE DEATHS	OTHER CAUSES	TOTAL
Revolution	4,435	. . . . . .	4,435
War of 1812	2,260	. . . . . .	2,260
Mexican War	1,733	. . . . .	1,733
Spanish American	385	2,061	2,446
World War I	53,407	63,156	116,563
World War II	293,986	113,842	407,828
Korean War	33,629	20,617	54,246
	389,835	199,676	589,511
Civil War	204,000	414,152	618,152
Union forces	110,070	250,152	360,222
Confederate forces	94,000	164,000 †	258,000

As is apparent from the above, figures on deaths from nonbattle causes of the first three wars are not available. But if it be assumed that nonbattle deaths were

---

* Compiled from Thomas Livermore, *Numbers and Losses in the Civil War,* and William Fox, *Regimental Losses in the Civil War.* Both books are outdated, but their figures are the best available.
† This estimate of nonbattle deaths on the Confederate side is too low, but there is insufficient information for an accurate revised estimate.

twice as numerous as battle deaths (as was roughly the situation in the Civil War), this would add a total of 16,856 deaths, distributed thus:

FIRST THREE WARS	ESTIMATED DEATHS OTHER CAUSES	ADJUSTED TOTALS
Revolution	8,870	13,305
War of 1812	4,520	6,780
Mexican War	3,466	5,199
	16,856	

The grand total of deaths in conflicts other than the Civil War thus becomes 589,511 plus 16,856 or 606,367

As these figures indicate, the principal killer of Civil War participants was not battle but sickness. The number of Yanks and Rebs who died of disease was more than twice the number who died of battle causes. The great prevalence of disease and the shockingly high death rate among those stricken by sickness, resulted from a combination of factors. First, the fact that a majority of the men were rural meant that many, if not most, of them had not previously been exposed to measles and other diseases common among urban children. When they were crowded into camp these contagious maladies struck with epidemic force and the victims, unaware of the danger, did not take proper care of themselves, and many developed complications that proved fatal.

A second reason for the frequency and deadliness of disease was ignorance of both cause and treatment on the part of physicians and patients. Bacteriology was an undeveloped science. Malaria and other illnesses were attributed to "miasms" arising from the lowlands and poisonous vapors permeating the atmosphere. Largely be-

cause of ignorance, sanitation and other safeguards against the contraction and spread of infectious disease were grossly inadequate.

A third cause of the widespread susceptibility to sickness was diet. Camp fare was usually deficient in fruits and vegetables, and milk was very difficult to obtain. This was especially true on the Confederate side, and the frequency of Johnny Reb's complaints of suffering from "the sh-ts" afforded abundant evidence of his dietary deficiencies.

And finally on both sides filth contributed greatly to dysentery and other maladies that plagued the camps. Most Yanks and Rebs thought only of convenience when disposing of waste and responding to the call of nature. A Reb wrote in his diary December 8, 1863: "On rolling up my bed this morning I found I had been lying in . . . something that didn't smell like milk and peaches." Refuse and offal accumulating in and around camps attracted hordes of flies that crawled over food and spread germs far and near. An Alabamian wrote his wife in June 1862: "There are more flies

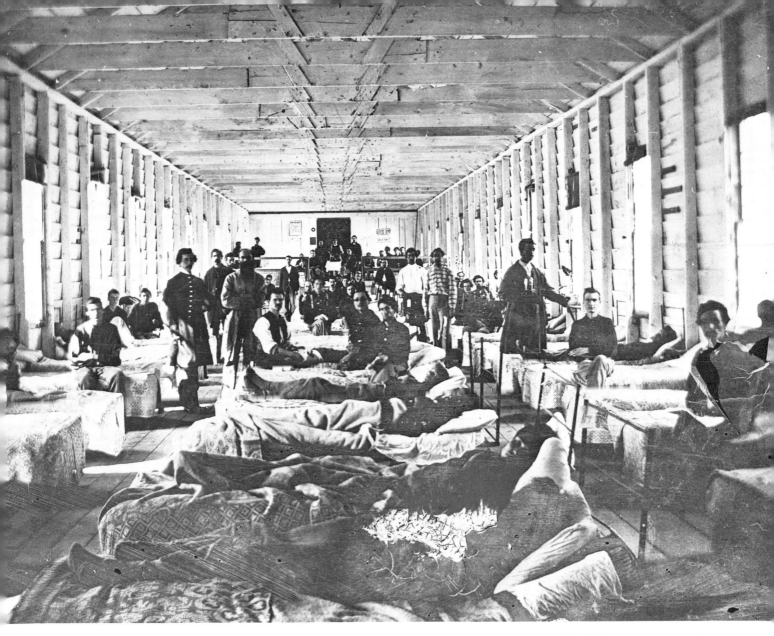

Hospitals like this were unknown in the early months of the war.
U.S. Signal Corps photo, National Archives.

here than I ever saw any where before, sometimes I . . . commence killing them but as I believe forty come to everyone's funeral I have given it up as a bad job." Germ-spreading mosquitoes, fleas, and body lice tormented soldiers even more than flies. A New Englander stationed in Louisiana wrote his homefolk in 1863: "We are in sore trouble with poisonous animals in the water, fleas on the ground and mos-

quitoes in the air." About the same time a Pennsylvanian encamped near Fredericksburg, Virginia wrote his brother: "I do not believe [that after Antietam] there was a man in our brigade, officer, private or nigger, but was lousy."

Medical reports show an aggregate of 6,029,564 cases of sickness on the Union side. Confederate records are incomplete, but if illnesses were half as numerous

Double amputee,
a private of the 147th New York.
Courtesy Wendell W. Lang, Jr.,
Tarrytown, New York.

among Southerners as among the Federals (who outnumbered them by more than two to one), as they undoubtedly were, cases on both sides totaled something over 9,000,000. The most common maladies were "looseness of the bowels" (diarrhea, dysentery, "flux," and scurvy), and measles and malaria (generally called "the shakes"). Pneumonia, smallpox, yellow fever, and tuberculosis were of less frequent occurrence, but all of them took a heavy toll of lives. The principal killers on both sides were typhoid and intestinal infections. Typhoid probably was responsible for one-fourth of all deaths from disease among

Civil War participants. On the Confederate side, and possibly among Federals as well, as many soldiers died of what they called "the sh-ts" as were killed in combat.

Civil War surgeons, reflecting the scientific backwardness of their time, often did their patients more harm than good. They amputated limbs and probed wounds with dirty instruments, dosed diarrhea patients with whiskey and strong purgatives and bled both sick and wounded with lancet or leech. The victims of such ministrations were quick to denounce their tormentors. An Ohioan wrote from near Vicksburg in March 1863: "hell will be Filde with doters and offersey when this war is over," and one Reb complained that "the Doctors kill more than they cour" while another rated surgeons as the "most unworthy of all the human famaly."

It is not meant to suggest that medical practices in Civil War armies were uniformly bad or that surgeons were universally incompetent, for such was not the case. Lessons learned from war experience and experimentation led to some decided improvements: notably in evacuating battle casualties; in transporting the wounded from combat zones by rail and ship; in de-

veloping pavilion type hospitals; and, on the Confederate side, especially, in improvising substitutes for scarce drugs. Particularly outstanding were the achievements of Doctors Samuel H. Stout and Joseph Jones on the Confederate side and of Doctors William A. Hammond and Jonathan Letterman among the Federals. Even so, the plight of Rebs and Yanks who were sick or wounded was generally terrible and the suffering that they endured exceeded that of participants in other American wars.

A Union field "hospital" during the Peninsular Campaign.
A white-hatted doctor in the foreground examines a wound.
Library of Congress.

The Call to Battle

THE editor and writer on modern warfare Ralph Ingersoll aptly noted that for soldiers in World War II "the battle is the payoff." He might well have said the same of Johnny Rebs and Billy Yanks, for closing with the enemy was for most the principal reason for entering the service and the climactic episode of their army experience. Generally they contemplated initiation into combat with a mixture of eagerness, nervousness, and dread. A Tennessee Reb wrote in his diary of his baptism of fire at Williamsburg, May 5, 1862:

I was not much surprised when we received the order to fall in. . . . I can never forget my thoughts as I stood there and looked around. . . . It was the first time I had ever

been called upon to face death. I felt in a few moments some of us standing here, vainly trying to jest and appear careless, would be in eternity. . . . The feeling called *fear* did not enter my breast, but it was painful, nervous anxiety, a longing for action . . . and a dull feeling about the chest that made breathing difficult. All the energies of my soul seemed concentrated in the one desire for action. We were not kept long in suspense for very soon orders came for us to go forward. . . . We advanced slowly . . . when the crack of a rifle and the falling of a man announced to us that we were in the range of the enemy's sharpshooting.

A Mississippian wrote his sweetheart in June 1862, after his first fight near Corinth: "I am glad to say that i was not scarde though i felt sorter curies. . . . though i did not run i mite have if i had thought of it in time." Concerning his baptism of fire at Shiloh another Mississippian wrote in his diary:

We are moving in line of battle cautiously and slowly. I have the shakes badly. Well I am not alone—in fact we all look like the shaky Quackers. Scared? Oh, no; only an old fashioned rigor. . . . Oh how I wish I was a dwarf, just now, instead of a six-footer.

A Yank anticipating his first fight wrote his father: "I have a marked dread of the battle field, for I . . . have never seen a person die . . . & I am afraid that the groans of the wounded & dying will make me shake nevertheless I hope & trust that strength will be given me to stand & do my duty."

OPPOSITE.
Union troops awaiting call to combat.
National Archives.

So great was the anxiety of soldiers awaiting their baptism of fire that when finally they entered into battle they experienced a sense of relief. "With your first shot you become a new man," wrote a Reb after First Manassas. "Fear has no existence in your bosom. Hesitation gives way to an uncontrollable desire to rush into the thickest of the fight. . . . You become cool and deliberate, and watch the effect of bullets . . . and [cannon] balls as they rake their murderous channels through your ranks . . . with a feeling so callous . . . that your soul seems dead to every sympathizing . . . thought." A similar reaction was experienced by a Massachusetts private who wrote his mother after his first battle: "As . . . the bullets began to whiz about us, I thought to myself, 'now the test is coming' & I wondered if I should meet it bravely. I nerved myself up . . . and moved forward at the command, expecting to be hit. . . . After the first round the fear left me and I was as cool as ever I was in my life." Another Yank, reporting his first encounter with Rebs, wrote his father: "Dear Pa . . . Went out a Skouting yesterday. We got to one house where there were five secessionists, they broke & run and Arch holored out to shoot the ornery suns of biches and wee all let go at them. They may say what they please, but godamit Pa it is fun."

The seasoning that came after their first exposure to combat enabled Yanks and Rebs to go into battle with less anxiety about "playing the coward," and with increasing indifference to the fate of their comrades. Many gained composure by taking the fatalistic view that every man had an appointed time to die and until that time arrived life was secure regardless of

Battle of Fredericksburg. Library of Congress.

the fury of enemy fire. Religiously inclined soldiers tended to interpret successive battle survivals as evidence to God's purpose to see them safely through the war. But the dread of battle lingered on in the minds of most soldiers and in some it increased, owing largely to a belief that luck could not last always and that they would be victims of the law of averages. The metamorphosis experienced by many veterans on both sides was vividly expressed by a Georgian of Lee's army, in a letter of November 19, 1864 to his wife:

I do not know what is getting into me but I am getting more and more scary every fight I go into. . . . In the first two or three engagements I shared in, I felt a sort of exultation in moving about unhurt when others about me were shot down, but all that seems to be done away with now & I am getting . . . as nervous about the whistling of bullets as any person I know of & I actually *suffer* when going into a fight, particularly when I have been looking forward to it for several days. Fortunately this feeling wears off very rapidly when once really in for it.

Both in their baptisms of fire and in their subsequent battles the experiences and reactions of soldiers varied greatly. Representative of the actions and impressions of many Civil War soldiers in many engagements were those recorded by the 16-year-old Private William H. Brearley of the 17th Minnesota, after Antietam, his second battle, and by Private Edmund D. Patterson, age 20, in the wake of his fourth fight, Gaines's Mill. On September 26, 1862, Brearley wrote:

It was rather strange music to hear the balls Scream within an inch of my head. I had a bullet strike me on the top of the head just as I was going to fire and a piece of Shell struck my foot—a ball hit my finger and another hit my thumb. I concluded they meant me. the rebels played the mischief with us by raising a U.S. flag. we were ordered not to fire and as soon as we went forward they opened an awful fire from their batteries on us we were ordered to fall back about ½ miles, I staid behind when our regiment retreated and a line of skirmishers came up—I joined them and had a chance of firing about 10 times more—in about an hour we had to fall back to the regiment—it was then about 6 P.M. I have heard and seen pictures of battles—they would all be in line all standing on a nice level field fighting, a number of ladies taking care of the wounded &c. &c. but it isent so, much, in both of these battles the rebels had Stone walls to get behind and the woods to fall back in. Our generals say they (the rebels) had as strong a position as could *possibly* be and we had to pick into them through an old chopping all grown up with bushes so thick that we couldent hardly get through—but we were so excited that the "old scratch" himself couldent have stopt us. We *rushed* on them evry man for himself—all loading & firing as fast as he could see a rebel to Shoot at—at last the rebels began to get over the wall to the rear and run for the woods. the firing encreased tenfold then it sounded like the rolls of thunder and all the time evry man shouting as loud as he could— I got rather more excited than I wish to again. I dident *think* of getting hit but it was almost a miricle that I wasent the rebels that we took prisoners said that they never before encountered a regiment that fought so like "Devils" (so they termed it) as we did—every one praised our regiment—one man in our company was Shot through the head no more than 4 feet from me he was killed instantly. after the battle I took care of the wounded until 11 P.M. I saw some the horidest sights I ever saw—one man had both eyes shot out—

Henry Lovie's sketch of a soldier falling in the midst
of battle at Munfordsville. New York Public Library.

and they were wounded in all the different
ways you could think of—the most I could do
was to give them water—they were all very
thirsty. . . . I was so dry at one time I could
have drank out of a mud puddle—without
stopping to ask questions—Our Colonel . . .
is just as cool as can be, he walked around
amongst us at the battle the bullets flying all
around him—he kept Shouting to us to fire
low and give it to them.

After the action at Gaines's Mill, near
Richmond, June 27, 1862, Private Patterson
wrote in his diary:

About five o'clock in the evening the order
was given; "Forward Guide, Center March,
Charge Bayonets." Up to the crest of the hill
we went at a double quick, but when we came
into view on the top of the ridge we met such

a perfect storm of lead right in our faces that the whole brigade literally *staggered* backward several paces as though pushed by a tornado. The dead lay in heaps, and two minutes in that position would have been utter annihilation. Just one moment we faltered, then the cry of Major Sorrell, "Forward Alabamians, —Forward!", and the cry was taken up by the officers of the different regiments and we swept forward with wild cheers over the crest and down the slope, and though at every step

some brave one fell, we did not falter. Just as we reached it [a deep ravine] we poured a volley into the front lines of the Yankees, and then some of the more active cleared it at a bound; others jumped in and scrambled up the opposite side. Immediately in front of me was a log or piece of timber thrown across. I crossed on it as did many others.

By the time we had gotten across, the front line, broken by our fire, frightened by our screams which sounded like forty thousand

Confederates capture DeGress's battery in the Battle of Atlanta, July 22, 1864. Library of Congress.

127

Confederate dead along the rail fence beside the Hagerstown Pike at Antietam. Library of Congress.

wild cats, had reached their second line and thrown them into confusion, and they, panic-stricken, left their works and crowded to the top of the hill, thus preventing their artillery from firing into us, and then commenced a scene that only the pen of an Abbot or a Victor Hugo could describe. The assaulting column consisted of six brigades, ours occupying the extreme right of the line, and each brigade had been successful. And the enemy, completely routed at every point, now lost all order and every man only thought of saving himself. They threw down their arms and ran in one grand mass, out of the woods and down the valley beyond. In vain their officers tried to rally them; they could not stand the terrible fire poured into them. We ran over their artillery, killing the gunners at their guns, and as this confused mass of fugitives

fled down the long open valley we kept close to them and shot them down by the hundreds and thousands. We were so close to them that pistol did as much good as guns, and we could not miss them for they were at least twenty deep, and very few of them offering to fire a shot.

By the time we had gone half a mile we were as much confused as the Yankees, for no one had paid any attention to company or regiment, but each had devoted his entire attention to loading and firing as fast as possible. At this critical juncture a large body of the enemy's cavalry appeared on the field, bearing down upon us. Quickly we closed our ranks and presented a pretty good front to the enemy, not such a line as would have stood an infantry charge, but plenty strong to resist cavalry. When the head of their columns had

Mangled dead soldier. Library of Congress.

gotten within about fifty yards of us we gave them a well directed and murderous fire that emptied many a saddle, and sent them flying in the opposite direction. . . .

The sun had set looking through the dust and smoke and fire of the battlefield, of a blood red color. We had won a complete victory, and now the scattered remnants of the various regiments and brigades that had been engaged had nothing to do except care for the wounded and to concentrate, that is, each man to find his proper command.

I did not know how tired I was until the excitement of the battle was over. I was almost too weak to stand, and my cheeks as hollow as though emaciated by a long spell of sickness. I dropped down under a bush and slept such a sleep as comes only to a tired soldier after a battle.

As soon after battle as convenient, most Rebs and Yanks wrote the folk at home to relieve apprehensions about their fate and to share experiences with loved ones. Typical of many communications was that written by a Hoosier on October 9, 1862, the day after Perryville:

Dear Wife I seat myself on the ground with a drum for a writing desk to write you a few lines to let you know that i am yet on top of the soil and not hirt. . . . There was plenty of men killed on both sides of me and not a ball struck me, the nearest I came to being hit was with a cannon ball it knocked me down it came so close to my head . . . but it did not hurt me much. . . . I should like to give you a description of the fight if i had the time and space but i havent either. . . . The rebels lost more than we did about two to one. . . . I was sent on the battle feild the next morning to take water to the wounded . . . and it was an awful sight to see there men torn all to pieces with cannon balls and bom shells the dead and wounded lay thick in all directions.

When telling homefolk of their battle experiences Yanks and Rebs sometimes alluded to the combat performance of their foes. When they conceded gallantry to the enemy they usually did so grudgingly. An Indianian, for instance, wrote his sweetheart after the fight at Ezra Church, near Atlanta, July 28, 1864: "The rebels were nearly every man drunk and some of the prisoners taken were so much intoxicated that they had to be led." But occasionally they revealed unstinted admiration of the courage displayed by their opponents. Fol-

lowing a sharp encounter near Richmond in May 1864, a New Yorker wrote:

Two full regiments of rebs . . . made a rush at us from the woods. . . . You should have seen the rascals, as clad in their threadbare suits of gray with short jackets . . . tight stockings, slender shanks and enormous yells and gesturing they advanced like so many crazy demons. Jer-usa-lem. What a storm of bullets they let fly at us. Overpowered we fell back double quick across a plowed field to the cover of a wood but quickly rallied and charged forward again with a hearty old Union cheer. Johnny Reb peppered and we peppered. Our fellows dropped fast. At length the secesh [sobriquet applied to Secessionists by Union men] got a crossfire on us . . . and we were scattered a second time.

Many soldiers commented on the confusion and the noise of battle. After Fredericksburg a Minnesota sergeant reported that before the end of the day's fighting his regiment was "scattered from Hell to Breakfast," and a Georgian who was at Malvern Hill wrote his aunt: "I never heard such a noise in all my life. It sounded like a large can[e] break on fire and a thunder storm with repeated loud thunder claps one clap following another." Ten days after the Williamsburg fight of May 5, 1862, a Minnesota sergeant wrote his sister: "The air perfectly whistled, shrieked and hummed with the leaden storm. . . . So loud [was] the rattle of musketry we could not hear the artillery."

Some recalled humorous incidents of battle, such as Rebel private Joseph Adams losing his pants from a shell burst at Murfreesboro and M. D. Martin having his two haversacks of hardtack fragmented by a cannon ball at Chancellorsville and scatter-

Dead Union soldiers lie thick before Battery Robinett
at Corinth, Mississippi, October 4, 1862. Library of Congress.

Two of Ewell's men who fought their last battle at Spotsylvania. Library of Congress.

ing crackers in such profusion that "several of the boys were struck by the biscuits and more than one thought he was wounded."

Lingering uppermost in the minds of most participants was the gruesomeness of battle, and incidents of horror and tragedy received major emphasis in letters to loved ones. "You doant no what kind of a-feeling it put on me to see men shot down like hoges & See a man tore all to peases with a Shell after he is dead," wrote a Georgian to his wife after the Battle of Chickasaw Bluffs; and another Georgian who walked over the field following Lee's victory at Chancellorsville reported: "It looked more like a slaughter pen than anything else. . . . The shrieks and groans of the wounded . . . was heart rending beyond all description." A Mississippi cavalryman, recounting to his mother a sharp clash during the retreat from Shiloh stated: "I shot men . . . until my heart was sick at the slaughter. . . . One fellow made a pass at me with his bayonet and . . . in an instant I wheeled and shot him through the breast and he tumbled over like a beef."

After Gettysburg a Maine soldier wrote his parents: "I have Seen . . . men rolling in their own blood, Some Shot one place, Some another. . . . our dead lay in the road and the Rebels in their hast to leave dragged both their baggage wagons and artillery over them and they lay mangled and torn to pieces so that Even friends could not tell them. You can form no idea of a battle field . . . no pen can describe it. No tongue can tell its horror I hope none of my brothers will Ever have to go into a fight." An Ohio soldier who walked over the field of Antietam two days after the fight described the scene thus to his father:

The smell was offul . . . there was about 5 or 6,000 dead bodes decaying over the field and perhaps 100 dead horses . . . their lines of battle Could be run for miles by the dead they lay long the lines like sheavs of Wheat I could have walked on the boddes all most from one end too the other.

Horror and tragedy found most vivid expression in individual instances observed by the soldiers. S. L. Loving of the 3d Michigan wrote his sister of what he saw while strolling over the battlefield of Williamsburg: "In one instance a Michigander and an Alabamian [who had] thrust a bayonet through each other lay dead, [each] still grasping his bayonet. . . . A Catholic died with a cross in his hands, and some with a string of beads. . . . Another had undone his knapsack and taken out his Testament and died with it grasped in his hands . . . opened to some promise. Others . . . held letters from home . . . as though loath to part with the last messengers from loved ones." After Seven Pines a New Yorker wrote to his homefolk: "I saw [Confederate] Father & Son side by side wounded. They both died where they lay." A Confederate colonel in recounting the experience of the 5th Texas at Gettysburg stated: "There were two twin brothers belonging to Company C . . . [who] came up to where I was standing and commenced firing. In a moment one of them is shot down by my side. The other brother caught hold of him as he fell and gently laid him down on the ground, and as he did so, he also received a death shot."

Of all soldiers' commentaries on the horror of battle, the most moving is the following letter written to A. V. Montgomery of

Facsimile of the dying Montgomery's blood-spotted letter.
Museum of the Confederacy, Richmond, Virginia.

Camden, Mississippi, by his mortally wounded son.

Spottsylvania County, Va.
[May 10, 1864]

Dear Father

This is my last letter to you. I went into battle this evening as Courier for Genl Heth. I have been struck by a piece of Shell and my right shoulder is horeribly mangled & I know death is inevitable. I am very weak but I write to you because I know you would be delighted to read a word from your dying Son.

I know death is near, that I will die far from home and friends of my early youth but I have friends here too who are kind to me. My Friend Fairfax will write you at my request and give you the particulars of my death. My grave will be marked so that you may visit it if you desire to do so, but [it] is optionary with you whether you let my remains rest here or in Miss. I would like to rest in the grave yard with my dear mother and brothers but its a matter of minor importance. Let us all try to reunite in heaven. I pray my God to forgive my sins & I feel that his promises are true that he will forgive me and save me.

Give my love to all my friends. My strength fails me. My horse & my equipments will be left for you. Again a long farewell to you. May we meet in heaven.

Your dying son,
J. R. Montgomery.

The "Friend Fairfax" kept his promise, and his letter, dated May 15, 1864, is filed with that of Montgomery in the Museum of the Confederacy at Richmond. Fairfax's letter reveals that Montgomery was taken to the hospital in the field but the surgeons after examining his wounds decided that an operation would be useless. Montgomery lingered until the morning of the 14th of May 1864, when he died peacefully. "On the evening he was wounded," Fairfax wrote the bereaved father, "his strength was sufficient to write you a letter which I enclose. . . . I have never witnessed such an exhibition of fortitude and Christian resignation as he showed. . . . No word of complaint escaped his lips. . . . He retained his consciousness to the last."

Thus a brave boy died, and in this poignant record of his death he bore eloquent witness to the tragedy of the Civil War.

135

Conclusion

WHAT conclusions can be drawn from J. R. Montgomery's record and that of all the other common soldiers involved in the great American conflict of 1861–1865? The Civil War made enormous and unprecedented demands on the American masses. Never before or since was so much of hardihood, sacrifice, and suffering required of them. And the magnificent manner in which most of them acquitted themselves in their time of testing justified the faith that had been reposed in them by Thomas Jefferson and the other Founding Fathers. Their admirable conduct in the nation's greatest crisis proved the soundness of democratic government and convincingly affirmed the hope expressed by Lincoln at Gettysburg that "a new nation, conceived in Liberty and dedicated to the proposition that all men are created equal . . . can long endure."

Between the lines during a truce.
*Battles and Leaders
of the Civil War.*

INDEX

Numbers in boldface refer to illustrations

139

INDEX